THE GOSPEL GOES TO WORK

*GOD'S BIG CANVAS OF
CALLING AND RENEWAL*

Dr. Stephen R. Graves

Dr. Stephen R. Graves
The Gospel Goes To Work
[Revised Edition—2017]
Published by KJK Inc. Publishing
P.O. Box 9448
Fayetteville, AR 72703

Details in some anecdotes and stories have been changed to protect the identities of the persons involved.

Scripture quotations indicated by NIV taken from THE HOLY BIBLE, NEW INTERNATIONAL VERSION®, NIV® Copyright © 1973, 1978, 1984, 2011 by Biblica, Inc.® Used by permission. All rights reserved worldwide. Scripture quotations indicated by MSG taken from The Message. Copyright © 1993, 1994, 1995, 1996, 2000, 2001, 2002. Used by permission of NavPress Publishing Group.

ISBN 978-1-940794-17-4

Prepared in association with Edit Resource, LLC (editresource.com)

THE GOSPEL GOES TO WORK
GOD'S BIG CANVAS OF CALLING AND RENEWAL

"THE HARVEST IS PLENTIFUL, BUT
THE WORKERS ARE FEW.
ASK THE LORD OF THE HARVEST,
THEREFORE,
TO SEND OUT WORKERS
INTO HIS HARVEST FIELD."

– LUKE 10:2 NIV

INTRODUCTION

Every Christian on the planet falls into one of four categories regarding the gospel/work conversation.

+ Those who don't think the gospel has any relevance or place in everyday work life.
+ Those who think it does belong but believe its only footing is in the soft, private, attitude elements.
+ Those who want to take the gospel to work but find themselves confused, unmotivated, or alone in that aim.
+ Those who have discovered that the reach, power, and intent of the gospel can revolutionize any worker … doing any work … in any setting.

I remember having a breakfast meeting with a CEO in Chicago who said, "It's being involved in the rigor of the business world day in and day out that keeps my life of faith strong." After pondering his comment, I think I understood what he meant. The pressure, demands, and choices endemic to business require a transparency and authenticity in our faith not found in the routine of religion.

I have been hanging around the faith and work corner all of my adult life. At times I tried to add catalytic thinking and enthusiasm (like the *Life@Work* magazine of old or *PraxisLabs.org* of late). Other times I found myself researching and learning from the Scriptures, the thinkers of the past, and the leaders of the present. And other times, I simply sat down on a bench and just lingered, listened, and watched people of faith go to work every day. What a rich and challenging field trip it has been.

As we shift to the next generation leading in every aspect of work, I want to keep the conversation going by offering a few thoughts and frameworks to help Millennials discover the power, reach, and intent of the gospel going to work. At the same time I wish the veterans of faith and work would be open to a fresh framework that could trigger a new level of leadership and impact.

This book, like all my work, is written not from the pulpit or the classroom out but from the street back. In other words, my voice is that of a practitioner, not a preacher or professor. The voice is simple, useful, and (somewhat) regretfully tied to my southern roots. The style invites you to agree or disagree but not just numbingly glaze over through chunks of pages.

I'm hoping for a global reset around Luke 10:2—the famous verse about asking the Lord of the harvest to send out more workers into the field. Let's ask ourselves, *Who are the workers?* These people are so much more than just missionary recruits, which is what many of us assume. They're any and all Christians doing any kind of work with a redemptive edge. *What is the field?* It's not just places where obvious Christian ministry takes place. It's any place in our lives where good or bad can be done, and this most definitely includes our workplaces. *What is the harvest?* It's not just individual souls coming to faith. It's any means by which the true, the good, and the beautiful come to life.

We can be the answers to the prayer. *We* can be the worker and our job can be the field. My presence and my work can both be the harvest and produce the harvest. For in work zones all around the world, the rumbling of gospel movements can be heard. Industry by industry, community by community, the power, reach, and intent of the gospel are extended, changing people's lives.

I love the weekends. But I gotta tell you, I love the weekdays just as much. Somewhere back in my younger life the passion around taking the gospel to work grabbed me and has never released me. I hope this book can share a bit of that with you.

CHAPTER 1

GOD'S BIG CANVAS

> *"Christians are called to redeem entire cultures,*
> *not just individuals."* [1]
> —Charles Colson

JOHN—A FIFTY-something pastor and global church planter—was at a pastors' conference, part of a panel ready to answer questions in front of a large assembly of church leaders. The interviewer directed the opening question to John: "What was your greatest failure in your ministry career?"

John never saw that question coming. It threw him off balance. Who would want to start out a public event by admitting his greatest failure?

I don't know how most ministry leaders would answer this question. Maybe something like, "My greatest failure was addiction to pornography." Or perhaps, "I wish I had not sacrificed my family for ministry." Or even, "I got lazy in my later years."

John had something very different to say. After thinking for a moment, he confessed, "My greatest failure has been my inability to understand the power of the gospel as it relates to the details of everyday life."

Think about that answer.

Here is a man who has believed and preached the gospel story for decades. He has shepherded scores of people in their journey of faith. His current mission is helping to catalyze gospel movements in sixty-five pivotal cities of the world through church planting. John Hutchinson is in the full-time gospel business, as they say. So I have to ask, *If someone like John can fail to press the gospel into the details of everyday life, do the rest of us stand a chance?*

Perhaps at times you've had a nagging feeling that you're not consistently living out your faith. There are times and places in your life where you sense the gospel could have freer rein and bear greater fruit through you. You'd like to see that happen, but you're not sure what to do about it.

I know I have felt that way. The regret that John Hutchinson voiced resonates within me. I have spent a lot of time praying, reading, talking about, thinking about, and writing about how to engage the gospel more fully. And yet, like John, I often wonder if I've really understood and accessed the reach, power, and full intent of the gospel into all of life.

I look at it this way: This world is God's canvas on which He is painting the powerful gospel story. Often He uses imperfect artists such as you and me to hold the brushes and even paint some of the strokes. But, He wants the whole canvas colored—that is, He wants all of life to reflect His goodness. I immediately think of Vincent van Gogh's approach to painting, who said, "I dream of painting and then I paint my dream."[2]

I believe van Gogh was borrowing a model from our Maker. God imaged us in creation and now paints His purposes onto our canvas. But He needs the complete canvas to paint His full picture. It takes the entire canvas, not just a favorite corner, to capture His complete heart and full intentions. The gospel narrative needs implementation everywhere.

There are blank areas of the canvas where God still wants to portray His story. These are spots in your life and work that have become beachheads of sin and evil or at least aren't displaying the work of God. The remedy to such blank areas is the introduction of the gospel narrative in its full power, reach, and intent. Here is a pivotal question we will consider later in

"THIS WORLD IS GOD'S CANVAS ON WHICH HE IS PAINTING THE POWERFUL GOSPEL STORY."

the book, one that every Christian needs to answer honestly: "Where are the parts of my life and work that the gospel isn't appreciably affecting?"

This book is about *work* and the gospel. Not *ministry work* only, like my good friend John and other pastors and missionaries do, but *every kind of work*. I have written it for the truck driver and the accountant, for the franchise owner and the stage actor, for the corporate executive and the nonprofit founder, for the army colonel and the orthodontist, for the TV news anchor and the high school principal—for anyone who has a job or is looking for a job.

Work represents one of the largest areas on the canvas of life. It is where we spend most of the best hours of our days. It is where we impact the world most directly with the redemptive edges of the gospel. It is where the biblical images of salt, light, and sweet perfume show their most noticeable contribution. So in this book I want to focus on a specific issue: *What more can you and I do to engage the gospel through our work?*

Understanding and then embracing the reach, power, and intent of the gospel is a revolutionary insight, even for veterans of the faith. This book is for workers in the first 90 days of their first jobs, and for the CEO considering the final three legacy years before retirement. The gospel is for everyone, at every stage of life, in every context in the world. The gospel has revolutionary side effects to life and work when understood and implemented correctly.

I believe that for the most part our spiritual imagination is stunted or handcuffed to the same frameworks and the same conversation over and over. And when a person of faith takes the gospel to work and gets on board with what I will soon introduce as the baseline and the blue sky, powerful redemptive things begin to happen.

WHAT THE GOSPEL LOOKS LIKE IN ACTION

Today, the case study is one of, if not the greatest teaching tool at Harvard Business School and other top B schools around the country. Real-life stories of business in action seem to provide a better learning opportunity to wannabe business leaders than reams of abstract business theory.

Similarly, in the first century, stories and figures of speech (metaphors and similes) were undisputed must-have techniques for any teacher who had something to say that really needed to stick. Jesus and other effective teachers of His day used specific, vivid word images all the time.

I want to highlight four word images from the New Testament that picture for us how the gospel goes to work both in us and through us. These images do not come close to describing every possible way that the gospel goes to work. Yet the gospel can operate in these four ways for all workers in all workplaces performing all kinds of work. Through these images, we can get a jump-start on understanding how the gospel goes to work.

A DASH OF SALT

For so many people, life is bland. They are bored, uninspired, and stuck in routine and monotony. Even pleasure seeking has lost its thrill. They wonder, *What's the point of my life?*

Can that kind of dissatisfaction, once it has reached the level of disillusionment and discouragement, ever be changed? Absolutely. I would suggest the gospel was intended to inject energy, purpose, and life into every piece of our being. Jesus said to His followers,

You are the salt of the earth. But if the salt loses its saltiness, how can it be made salty again? It is no longer good for anything, except to be thrown out and trampled underfoot.[3]

Begin thinking now about how your work can help make others' lives more exciting, rewarding, and meaningful. That's the gospel adding a dash of salt to give a new tastiness to the dish of their life.

A RAY OF LIGHT

Immediately after calling His followers the salt of the earth, Jesus followed up with a second image:

You are the light of the world. A town built on a hill cannot be hidden. Neither do people light a lamp and put it under a bowl. Instead they put it on its stand, and it gives light to everyone in the house. In the same way, let your light shine before others, that they may see your good deeds and glorify your Father in heaven.[4]

The truth is, we live in a world that can be dark and confusing. Even the best of us can find ourselves in need of clarity, direction, and confidence. Have you ever unpacked the full intent of you being salt and light in a work place? Can you imagine how your work, and the way you go about doing it, can help to dispel the murk for others?

A DAB OF PERFUME

One of the great needs in this world is for people to realize their value and worth. So many don't think they're important. They don't think others could like them and want to be with them. They don't see that they have much to contribute.

Many work settings, quite frankly stink! They are a place where greed, bullying, dishonesty, and the like have been rooted and bore its nasty fruit. To counter that Paul says drop a dab of perfume on it? What does he mean? He means that a follower of Jesus should transform a stinky environment over time.

The apostle Paul said,

We are to God the pleasing aroma of Christ among those who are being saved and those who are perishing. To the one we are an aroma that brings death; to the other, an aroma that brings life.[5]

Does your work bring you into contact with people who think they are worthless or unlikable? Prepare to touch them with a gospel assuring them that, as people created in the image of God, they can be attractive and valuable.

A LUMP OF LEAVEN

People have a way of getting stuck. They aren't growing. They don't see movement. They aren't productive in the way they want to be. Even if externally it might appear to others that a lot is happening in their lives, on the inside they know that nothing that really matters is going on.

You may have felt that way yourself at one time. But if the gospel has gotten inside you, then you now experience motion and expansion.

Jesus used more than one growth metaphor in His teaching. Perhaps the most memorable is that of leaven, or yeast. In Jesus' day, bread makers would take a piece of older dough that already had some leaven in it, and then they would add it to a new batch of dough and leave the whole thing to sit for a while.

The leaven (a microorganism) would next spread through the whole dough, producing carbon dioxide bubbles that would cause the dough to rise. Instead of hard, unpalatable flat bread, you would have a soft and spongy loaf that was a pleasure to eat. And this makes it a metaphor of the gospel.

The kingdom of heaven is like yeast that a woman took and mixed into about sixty pounds of flour until it worked all through the dough.[6]

Leaven has a mysterious power to spread and create growth where there was none before. That's just what stuck people need—a jumpstart, a catalyst, a leavening agent to get inside them and initiate movement. Find a way to use your work to help others grow.

So this is what it looks like when the gospel goes to work:

+ It looks like excitement appearing where once there was boredom.
+ It looks like insight dawning where once there was confusion.
+ It looks like attractiveness showing up where once there was a barrier.
+ It looks like growth happening where once there was stagnation.

Does your understanding and approach to the gospel spread over to your work?

THREE WORKERS, ONE QUESTION

While writing this book, in the span of forty-eight hours I had three conversations that illustrated again just how common it is for people of faith to wrestle with being better kingdom citizens regarding their work. The situations these three people found themselves in were quite different, and consequently they nuanced their questions differently, but all three of them were basically asking the same question: *How can I take the gospel to work?* They may not have known it, but they wanted to be salt and light, perfume and leaven.

MARK (THE VETERINARIAN)

I was flying back from an annual fishing trip in remote Ontario, Canada when one of the guys in our group, Mark, started talking to me about what it means to be a Christian and a veterinarian.

Mark is 56 and has been a devout man of faith as long as I have known him. He has tried to follow the guidelines of Scripture in the way he lives his life and does his work. So this is not some new territory for him. But lately he has been wondering if he is missing out on a greater expression of the gospel going to work.

"How can I live for Christ with more impact in my veterinarian practice? And what things are missing to have a greater gospel footprint in my practice?" he asked me.

SCOTT (THE CEO)

After returning home from the fishing trip, I returned a call from a client who had left a phone message. His name is Scott.

Scott has been blessed to take over the family business. Mind you, he did more than just stay out of jail, inherit the CEO chair, and make daily runs to the bank with deposits. He has had to navigate a challenging period and has led the company through a huge growth season approaching a billion dollars.

Like Mark, he is not a newbie to the aspiration of engaging his faith more intentionally into his work. Since it is common for successful business owners to find themselves with personal resources to invest, Scott had been placing some "kingdom investments" for some time. He and his family have consistently given a huge percentage of their income and net worth over the last few years to all kinds of causes.

He asked me, "How do I spot a cause that has both a great kingdom impact and a strong financial return? In other words, what does a plus/plus investment really look like? How much risk should I take, and how should I sort all the opportunities coming my way?" He was dialing up the "gospel going to work" dialogue in a personal way to his particular giving strategy.

KILE (THE COLLEGE SENIOR)

Earlier that same day, my son, Kile, and I were having breakfast.

At the time Kile was a senior business major trying to figure out his work prospects after college. A great summer internship with a local company helped push his thinking forward. Thankfully, he has been infected, in a good way, with the desire to be involved in a business that is all about a multiple bottom line. And because his faith is core to his worldview and lifestyle, he wants to find a place where that is allowed or maybe even embraced.

"Does this mean I should work for a Christian company?" he asked me. "And what does it even mean for a company to be 'Christian' anyway? Can I have a kingdom impact working in a secular commercial company?"

A NEW WAY OF LOOKING AT FAITH ON THE JOB

The three workers I talked to all had legitimate questions. And although they were all different, in many respects they were all asking a similar shaping question: *How does the gospel go to work with me?*

With Mark, Scott, and Kile, I shared a framework for understanding the guidelines and possibilities of faith-work interaction. It's the framework I'll be getting to later in this book. I call it The Baseline and the Blue Sky Grid.

My promise to you at the outset is that this grid has the potential to marry your faith and your job in a way you've probably never experienced. It starts with practices that are easily within reach and then stretches as far as your spiritual imagination can soar. It will help you fill in the blank spaces of your canvas with the beauty and power of the gospel narrative. It will help you shove through the usual hesitations of "I work in a public company," "My boss is not a Christian," or whatever else may handcuff you to only a baseline embrace of the gospel's reach. It will help you spot the areas of your life that are untouched by the gospel and turn them into salt and light hot spots.

But first, I want to make sure your vision of the gospel is large enough to encompass the fullness of its drama. That's where it all begins when taking the gospel to work.

"THE BASELINE AND BLUE SKY
FRAMEWORK WILL HELP YOU
SPOT YOUR GOSPEL GAPS AND
TURN THEM INTO SALT AND
LIGHT HOT SPOTS."

CHAPTER 2

THE GOSPEL
AND YOUR JOB

"The gospel is like a caged lion. It does not need to be defended, it simply needs to be let out of its cage." [1]
—*Charles Spurgeon*

WHO YOU WORK for is more significant than what you do or where you work. That's a radical statement, I know. But I mean something perhaps different than what you are thinking at first. I am actually just paraphrasing what the apostle Paul says to workers in the first century, and I believe it applies to every worker doing any kind of work today—"Whatever you do, work at it with all your heart, as working for the Lord, not for human masters, since you know that you will receive an inheritance from the Lord as a reward. It is the Lord Christ you are serving."[2]

The reach, power, and intent of the gospel can revolutionize the work you do—regardless of what it is—when you realize that you are really working for Christ. Not for your earthly boss. Not for yourself and your family. Not for your colleagues or your customers. Not for the bonus. But instead, ultimately, for Jesus Himself.

I recently listened as a friend pondered the question "What exactly makes any work gospel-minded work?" Is it the product being sold? Is it that the overt gospel is shared and people come to marked faith at work? Is it a certain culture of values and beliefs encasing the organization? If you give someone a glass of water but don't share the gospel, is there any gospel activity taking place? We will get to all those, but I mean to underscore now that any work becomes gospel work when any worker "is working as unto Jesus."

A gospel-centered life is a *way*, not a destination or particular address. And gospel-minded work starts with my

"EVERY CHRISTIAN'S JOB DESCRIPTION BEARS AN APPENDIX-STAKING CLAIM BY THE GOSPEL OF JESUS."

mindset, my motivation, and my allegiance. Every Christian's job description bears an appendix-staking claim by the gospel of Jesus.

It is the Lord Christ you are serving.

That perspective changes our sense of purpose in our work life. It changes our motivation for working. It changes our attitude toward our job, both when things are going well and when they aren't. It changes our hopes and dreams about work. It reshapes and redeems what we hope to accomplish.

And so we need a view of the gospel that is large enough to encompass the promise that every career can be a calling. In other words, we need the *whole* gospel, not the incomplete gospel that sadly so many of us have bought into. The real gospel is what it will take to fill the full canvas of life with God's beauty.

RESTORING THE MISSING PIECES OF THE GOSPEL

I believe many Christians have been living with an abbreviated gospel without even knowing it.[3] For them, the drama of the gospel has just two acts: *Fall* and *Redemption*. The first of these acts goes like this: The world has been terribly messed up by sin, starting with the First Adam. And the second act follows with redemption by and in the Second Adam: Through believing in Jesus, you can be saved from your sin and accepted by the heavenly Father.

The two-act gospel is correct and marvelous … as far as it goes. But this gospel falls short of being the whole narrative. There are actually *four* acts in the drama of what God is accomplishing in human history. Fall and Redemption are, in reality, only acts II and III.

To understand the relationship between the gospel and work, we need to go back further in the handiwork of God and

THE TWO-ACT GOSPEL

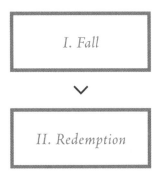

recognize that the first act is not Fall but *Creation.* Sure, we know that God created the universe, but do we really consider the importance of this fact? Since God chose to do the work of Creation and declared it "good," this shows us how much the world means to God. The reversal of human sin through divine forgiveness is not the only thing that matters. God created all things for a purpose.

Then, at the other end of the script, we need to recognize that the final act is not Redemption but instead *Renewal,* not our personal deliverance from sin only but rather God's restoration of all things. He is about the remaking of His fallen creation, and while this restoration won't be consummated until the end of history, it's in process now and we can have a part in it.

Makes a lot of sense, doesn't it?

But so what? Is it really such a big deal that we tend to lop off the opening and closing acts in the gospel drama?

It *is* a big deal. The type of gospel we believe in makes a difference because it affects how we think about our purpose

THE FOUR-ACT GOSPEL

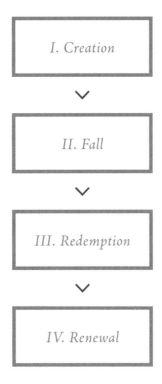

I. Creation

II. Fall

III. Redemption

IV. Renewal

in life. If we have a two-act gospel, we will probably see our role in life as being merely to help others find personal salvation in Jesus. But if we have a four-act gospel, we will be in the business of *both* helping individuals know Jesus *and* contributing to God's mission of renewing the world. It takes both to bring complete honor and glory to God. It takes both to paint His full story on the canvas of my life and work.

A while back, I was visiting with my friend Donnie. He is retired now, but back then he was still the very effective CEO of Tyson Foods. He spent time every year with his wife in Africa during his vacation. Mind you, they didn't go as tourists or as adventurous nomads. They weren't even going as traditional evangelist missionaries, but rather as intentional workers trying to live out the four-act gospel narrative.

Since I love a good field trip, I asked to see some pictures of their recent trip to Rwanda. As Donnie flipped through the pictures, he explained his partnership with his alma mater (the University of Tennessee) to build sustainable feed mills to help reverse the hunger crisis in Rwanda for generations to come. He came upon a scene of a mudslide and stopped to explain how the rainy seasons had eroded the rich topsoil needed to grow crops. He looked at me and said, "God cares about erosion, doesn't He?"

"You bet He does," I responded. The four-act gospel tells us He does.

The four-act gospel provides a comprehensive perspective of meaning for our lives, including our work.

A DUTY (AND A PRIVILEGE)

Moving from an incomplete two-act gospel to the full four-act gospel recalls a concept that previous generations knew about but that many of us in recent years have lost. Theologians call it the *cultural mandate*.

It goes all the way back to Genesis 1:26-28, where we read that God created the human race in His own image and told them to "fill the earth and subdue it" and to "rule over" the rest of creation. Note this was before the fall into sin and before God launched His rescue operation to redeem sinners. The *fill, subdue,* and *rule* command is a Creation mandate with lasting validity for all people in all times and places. Whenever people produce useful goods, create art that inspires, teach the young, protect the vulnerable, lead others in government or

"THE FOUR-ACT GOSPEL
PROVIDES A COMPREHENSIVE
GRID OF MEANING FOR OUR LIVES,
INCLUDING OUR WORK."

private organizations, engage in selling or banking or investing, or perform any number of other kinds of labor that produce order and value in human culture, they are obeying God's command to "Get busy making something out of this world I have created for you!"

This is a life-altering way of looking at your work:

If you realize that Creation is a part of God's great plan (Act I), then you realize that your particular field of work is a part of that plan too.

If you realize that Renewal is an aspect of what God is doing (Act IV), then you can see your work life as a partnership with Him in His work.

A four-act view of the gospel expands the canvas of calling and renewal.

Nancy Pearcey, in *Total Truth*, says this about the cultural mandate and work:

> *The lesson of the Cultural Mandate is that our sense of fulfillment depends on engaging in creative, constructive work. The ideal human existence is not eternal leisure or an endless vacation—or even a monastic retreat into prayer and meditation—but creative effort expended for the glory of God and the benefit of others. Our calling is not just to "go to heaven" but also to cultivate the earth, not just to "save souls" but also to serve God through our work. For God Himself is engaged not only in the work of salvation but also in the work of preserving and developing His creation. When we obey the Cultural Mandate, we participate in the work of God Himself.*[4]

Acting on these insights is not just a suggestion from God. It's a mandate. It's an order!

I've known people who had a two-act gospel and who believed that the only godly purpose they had in working was to help convert the unbelievers in their workplace. And what happens when everybody in their office becomes a believer? Well, from their perspective, they no longer have a spiritual reason for working there. But the four-act gospel provides a bigger picture.

I've known people who believed that the only way a person could truly do kingdom work was to work either in a ministry structure or for a company that produced a gospel product or service. The four-act gospel provides a bigger picture.

I hope these people will come to understand that the work itself is a service to God. The gospel is at work, not only when they share about Jesus with a non-Christian in the next cubicle, but also when they perform a service to humanity by doing something valuable in their work. The gospel is at work when they make choices about how to do their work so that their work is more consistent with God's values. This is a truth that's been lost to many but is in the process of being recovered.

DAVE AND DEMI'S EPIPHANY

Husband-and-wife couple Dave and Demi Kiersznowski are the owners of DEMDACO Corporation, producer of home décor products, including the popular Willow Tree line of figurines. The couple are also followers of Jesus who have learned to live out the gospel in their everyday lives, including their work.

Dave grew up believing that some people had vocations from God and others just had jobs. For a long time, he and Demi measured their success as Christians by how much money they were able to give away to their church and other good causes at the end of the year. They were living what I like to call the "do this so I can do that" model. Over time, though, their perspective changed. They discovered infinite possibilities for how to please God with their work, which included giving money away, but included much more than that too.

Dave explains, "We were missing the fact that our daily lives could be offered as a sweet aroma to God—that the ethos of our company could be a sweet offering to Him. We see that now."[5]

A part of the transformation that the Kiersznowskis went through was simply having their eyes opened to the fact that the work they were doing was in itself a service to God, simply because it had value to their customers and employees. Another part was an ongoing process of figuring out ways to maximize the gospel impact of their work.

Through DEMDACO, Dave and Demi create products designed to "lift the spirit," and they try to instill the same sense of positive purpose in their employees. For example, in their headquarters, they installed artwork by Makoto Fujimura, a painter who sees all of life through the lens of the Christian story. They also named the meeting spaces in their building after "heroes of the common good," such as Mother Teresa and Martin Luther King Jr., reminding employees that their labor can impact history. Together, they are all engaged in the pursuit of doing good for others. They discovered not only *what* they are going to do at work, but a new *way* to go about it.

Speaking for himself and his wife, Dave says, "We're so grateful that now, on Monday morning, we feel that we're doing what [God] specifically, uniquely made us to do, and that our company and our vocations need no other justification."[6]

The gospel has gone to work with the Kiersznowskis at DEMDACO.

ANY WORKER, ANY WORKPLACE, ANY WORK

Understanding and embracing the reach, power, and intent of the gospel can alter the way we consider our work and do our work. The gospel is supposed to thoroughly fill the canvas of our work experience. And when we allow the gospel to do its work through us, we can enjoy a sense of fulfillment and "rightness" in our work that we can have no other way.

What's your initial reaction to this statement?

If objections spring to your mind, trust me—I've heard a few of them before.

- "Yeah, but you don't know my boss and the people I work with. The last thing they're thinking about is God."
- "What do you mean, 'the gospel at work'? We don't make Bibles; we sell earth-moving equipment."
- "I'm in a public company. We're all about driving our stock price and producing profit."
- "From the chair where I sit, I don't have enough pull in the organization to shape how things are done."
- "The work we do is really boring and ordinary, and I only took the job because I needed the money."
- "I'm no theologian. I wouldn't know where to start."

If you have an objection like these, I understand your hesitation. It's not always apparent how the gospel can go to work.

But I want you to stick with me, because if there's one thing I've learned, it's that the applicability of God's truth is bigger than your own context. You don't have to wait for certain conditions to exist before the gospel can make a difference in your work. Wherever you are, whatever you are doing, the gospel matters.

What I say over and over again is that the gospel can travel with *any worker* and can be active in *any workplace* and applied to *any work*. This is true regardless of the particulars of your job. This is true regardless of your Myers-Briggs personality profile, and it is true whether you are in your first year of work or your last year. The gospel can change your work life whether you're an accountant in Michigan, a salesman in San Diego, a computer programmer in the Pacific Northwest, or a football coach in the Southeastern Conference.

I'm going to give you a framework for understanding how to do this when I introduce The Baseline and the Blue Sky Grid in Chapter 4. But on the way to doing that, I want to underscore why taking the gospel to work is

+ strategic,
+ timely, and
+ life changing for you.

"THE GOSPEL CAN TRAVEL
WITH ANY WORKER AND CAN
BE ACTIVE IN ANY WORKPLACE
AND APPLIED TO ANY WORK."

CHAPTER 3

WHY FAITH AT WORK MATTERS

"I asked that [work] should be looked upon, not as a necessary drudgery to be undergone for the purpose of making money, but as a way of life in which the nature of man should find its proper exercise and delight and so fulfill itself to the glory of God." [1]
—Dorothy Sayers

MANY YEARS AGO, back when I was in college, I first encountered the books of Francis Schaeffer. This American-born theologian living in Switzerland didn't refer specifically to the gospel as having four acts, as we saw in the last chapter, but he taught the similar idea that our faith should affect every part of what we do. I was immediately captivated. For me, as a young man who had been raised with the two-act gospel, Schaeffer's bigger vision opened my eyes to a new way of living as a Christian. I even thought for a while about joining his community in Switzerland called L'Abri.

I never moved to Switzerland, but I did pursue a theological education in the United States. I did so, not because I necessarily intended to become a pastor, but because Francis Schaeffer showed me how a knowledge of faith would provide bedrock grounding for any career I might choose. I knew that if I were looking for a fulfilling life, whatever my vocational future, I needed for my conversation about God to be right in the middle of it.

Schaeffer and other thinkers so persuaded me that faith can and should be integrated with all aspects of life that, in the years that followed, I became scandalized when I noticed Christians overlook the role of work in honoring God. Let me give you an example.

In the heyday of Focus on the Family, I visited the

organization's headquarters in Colorado Springs. Inside the building, I saw a plaque that read, "God ordained three institutions: family, government, and church." No doubt, with this statement, the people at Focus were trying to elevate the importance of family—a great goal, of course. But I said to myself, *Hmm, something seems to be missing. What about work?*

Work is not a curse from the Fall. Many Christians recognize that family is a pre-Fall institution, while assuming that work is a *post*-Fall institution. In other words, they think that work is something we do because we have to. It was not something that God originally intended for us, they think, and it doesn't have an important role in His eternal plan.

That could not be more wrong.

Now, it's true that after the Fall, work changed—it became harder and less satisfying.[2] But God ordained work for the human race from the very beginning. As we've seen, He gave us a cultural mandate to adapt the materials of the world He had made.[3] In addition, He issued Adam a business card naming him as "Caretaker, Garden of Eden."[4] All of this tells us that we have a God-given role in creating beautiful and useful things for the betterment of humankind, anticipating God's ultimate restoration of all things.

Those who pick up on the effect that sin has had on work often grow cynical and focus on how meaningless and mundane work can be. Intuitively, they know work (because hard Mondays, grumpy bosses, fields flooded with parasites, bear markets, etc.) is not as it should be. But they have a gap in their canvas. The third and fourth acts of the gospel give us hope. God is renewing and restoring work, not just to the way it was in Act I, but even better than ever before! God put work at the beginning *and* the end of His story—work is in the Garden, and it's in the New Jerusalem.

I would argue that the message about the gospel's integration with work is needed as much now as it ever has been, if not more so. Let me give you three reasons why I think this message is important to you.

1. WORK IS WHERE WE SPEND MOST OF OUR TIME.

According to polling data, Americans who have full-time jobs spend an average of forty-seven hours per week doing their work.[5] That makes it our single largest use of time, with sleep as the only close runner-up.[6] Whether work *should be* taking up that much of our time is a debate for another day. But undeniably, most adults spend most of their peak productive hours working. You know that from daily experience.

So let me ask you:

+ Why would we want to exclude the largest piece of our lives from serving Jesus?
+ Doesn't it make more sense to see our work hours as an immense opportunity to live out our faith—a vast region on the canvas of life?

I'll put it another way: *Work is core to our lives.* And, *the gospel is core to our faith*. Neither is a peripheral matter. So when we figure out how to align our work with the gospel, our lives become focused like never before.

Sure, it's possible to compartmentalize your life—work over here, faith over there. But it's far better to break down all the walls between the compartments and let the gospel spill over into every area of our lives, as it was always meant to do.

Work frames, contains, and covers so much of our life. We need to bring the gospel to bear within it.

"WORK IS CORE TO OUR LIVES. AND, THE GOSPEL IS CORE TO OUR FAITH. NEITHER IS A PERIPHERAL MATTER. SO WHEN WE FIGURE OUT HOW TO ALIGN OUR WORK WITH THE GOSPEL, OUR LIVES BECOME FOCUSED LIKE NEVER BEFORE."

2. THE WORLD OF WORK IS CHANGING.

Business books and magazines, leadership conferences, for-profit and nonprofit management courses, and lots of popular news articles and casual conversations agree about one thing: the nature of our work is different from what it used to be. *Fast Company* has a whole section of its magazine called "Generation Flux," whose tagline is "Modern business is pure chaos."[7] Hyperbole, but not by much.

My point is this: work is changing, so the way that the gospel rides with a worker must change too.

THE WORKER IS CHANGING

The incoming generation—the Millennials—don't care about work in the same way that, say, Baby Boomers did. For Boomers (now retiring at a fast pace), work was at the undisputed center of the plate. For Millennials, though, while work is definitely *on* the plate, so is a lot of other stuff. They want their jobs organized in such a way that they can participate in everything that matters to them.

This is just one way that the worker is changing.

Here's another example: contract labor is growing even among the most professional verticals. So today's worker often isn't even an employee.

The evolution of the American worker is taking place before our eyes.

THE WORK SETTING IS CHANGING

What fueled the rise of coffee shops across the land? For one thing, it was the desire so many people had to work outside their offices. Wi-fi–connected laptops and cell phones made it possible to work from a bistro table with a caramel macchiato steaming at your fingertips. Beats a cubicle!

Early on, Starbucks stores had little or no seating, because they wanted to get customers in and out fast. When they added seating, though, they found that their customer numbers exploded. These stores had, in effect, become offices.

That's just a start.

When people do work in offices, factories, and warehouses, they increasingly expect an environment designed for sustainability. Many work from home. The nine-to-five workday is a dinosaur. These are just some of the ways that the workplace or work setting looks different than it used to.

THE WORK ITSELF IS CHANGING

Who had even heard of app developers a generation ago? How many social media managers did you know back then? How many cloud-computing experts?

And it's not just tech that's changing. Not long ago, I met someone who had built up a substantial business walking dogs. I thought, *Wow, who would have thought there was money in that?* But this person had found that niche and done well with it.

Meanwhile, once-familiar positions that people held—like bank tellers, travel agents, sewing machine operators, and file clerks—will perhaps one day join the ranks of bygone workers such as switchboard operators.

WORKING GOES ON, BUT THE WORK CHANGES

The world of work has always been in flux to some extent, but the rate of change has sped up. That means we face increasing pressure to adapt the gospel for the new conditions of work. The way Christians of the past took the gospel to work may not be successful anymore. On the other hand, new opportunities for representing the gospel at work may exist today that previous generations could not have imagined. And a few years (or just months) from now, conditions will have changed again!

Just as global missionaries contextualize the gospel for their field, so you have to learn to translate and apply the gospel to your work as it exists today. And keep on contextualizing it.

This imperative is really nothing new.

God incarnated (fleshed out) Himself in Jesus to bring the gospel into the world. Since then, Jesus' followers have had to figure out how to incarnate the gospel in their environment. For example, the apostle Paul said, "I have become all things to all people so that by all possible means I might save some. I do all this for the sake of the gospel."[8] When he was in Athens, Rome, or Jerusalem, whether he was with Jews or Gentiles, Paul was willing to adapt and adjust to spread the gospel.

The gospel itself never changes. But as it lends itself to endless applications, it remains ever fresh and powerful.

3. WE OFTEN OPERATE OUT OF MENTAL "BAD BOXES" ABOUT WORK.

A Wall Street investment banker found himself growing weary of his work. Even though he was only in his thirties, he told me he wanted to quit work and retire. He had the money to do it. And if he did, he would be fulfilling the daydream many of us have had.

Yet, in my role as his executive coach, I advised against it. I urged him to take time off and craft a vision for where he might flex his commercial muscles during the next season of his life. He didn't have to keep doing what he was doing, but he shouldn't give up on work.

He wouldn't listen to me. He quit his job and said, "I will never work again."

I didn't believe him. Life would teach him that he had made

"THE GOSPEL ITSELF
NEVER CHANGES. BUT
AS IT LENDS ITSELF TO
ENDLESS APPLICATIONS, IT
REMAINS EVER FRESH AND
POWERFUL."

---

a mistake, I was sure. So I bet him that he'd be back at work within eighteen months.

It wasn't long before I collected on that bet—all $20.

This man was operating out of a mental "bad box." He let his temporary weariness make him overlook the fact that human beings are hardwired by our Maker to work.

While you and I may not make that particular mistake, we most likely have our own bad boxes when it comes to work. In many different ways, our view of work can be broken. We people of faith make work out to be something it is not, and in the process we let ourselves be handcuffed by our misunderstanding of work. Yet work remains a fundamental part of God's spiritual economy.

Consider the following three common ways in which Christians operate out of a bad box when it comes to thinking about work. Do any of these sound familiar to you, or make you think of other ways in which you take an unbiblical view of work?[9]

Bad Box 1: Work is enemy territory.

For those with this misunderstanding, work is part of the secular world, not to be confused with the sacred world. "God stuff" includes such things as prayer, Bible study, worship services, and donations of time and money to worthy "ministries." Work is secular.

This approach is totally counter to Scripture. This dichotomy—the split between the sacred and secular—doesn't occur in God's Word. In fact, Scripture spends a good deal of ink and paper making the point that these two should be tied together—that work is part of God's everyday involvement with people.

Bad Box 2: Work is salvation.

For people who buy into this myth, work becomes God. They don't go to work; they go to Work. They don't seek success; they seek Success. They don't have ambition; they have Ambition. Their entire identity becomes wrapped up in their job.

This is a particularly dangerous side of any "our company is family" culture. Many organizations, religious or otherwise, sell a family-oriented culture as a benefit. And it can be. Yet people who take this idea to the extreme can become emotional and spiritual prisoners to their jobs as a substitute for an intimate connection to their Maker.

The truth is that work is a great environment in which to discover God and to glorify God, but it is *not* God.

Bad Box 3: Work is a low priority.

Many followers of Christ, if asked to list their priorities, would order them this way: God, family, self, and work. But is this kind of ranking even biblical? Doesn't a holistic view of life see God as involved in every aspect of our lives?

Consider a new set of priorities for life: God. That's it. There is no number two or number three or number four. In living out a commitment to that priority, we must make Him an integrated part of everything we do—family, self, work, and everything else. This means we don't downgrade work in order to try to make God preeminent in our hearts.

Besides, relegating work to caboose status is as impractical as it is unbiblical. If we really put work last, we would not leave for work each day until we had done everything we should for God, family, and self. We'd never earn a living and we'd all be moving back home with our parents! No, the truth is that work is part of a balanced approach to life and God.

READY TO RECEIVE HEAVENLY PAINT

As I've said, your life and work is a big canvas on which God is painting the gospel story. Work does not make up the whole of that canvas, but it occupies a large area of it. I hope you are persuaded that you should be inviting God to intentionally paint in the work area of your life as in every other area.

What we need is a framework to help us evaluate how each of us individually can reflect the gospel well while succeeding at work and how the organizations we work for can be structured to serve as better channels for the gospel.

"YOUR LIFE AND WORK IS A
BIG CANVAS ON WHICH GOD IS
PAINTING THE GOSPEL STORY.
WORK DOES NOT MAKE UP THE
WHOLE OF THAT CANVAS, BUT IT
OCCUPIES A LARGE PART OF IT."

CHAPTER 4

THE BASELINE AND THE BLUE SKY

"It is not what a man does that determines whether his work is sacred or secular, it is why he does it. The motive is everything."[1]
—A. W. Tozer

FRAMEWORKS HELP US make sense of life. We use them every day when we drive through town or catch a subway, when we cook dinner or run through a pick-up line, and when we solve a problem or lay out a strategy. I want to introduce you to the most helpful and usable framework I have ever seen regarding the "gospel going to work" discussion. I call it The Baseline and the Blue Sky Framework.

The Baseline is the notion that every worker doing any kind of work is universally tethered to certain mindsets and behaviors, with no exception. It is the non-negotiables, the bare minimum any worker of faith should embrace regarding their job. The Blue Sky is the opposite. It represents the boundless horizon of what could be when I personalize the gospel to my personality and calling and the particular work setting I work in. It is me saying I have this background and wiring and work in a public company or for an unbelieving boss—then figuring out your specific path of greatest impact.

I have little doubt that you're already familiar with the idea of a baseline and the blue sky in general. But have you applied them to the way the gospel goes to work with you? These two concepts—baseline and blue sky—have the power to transform your work life in a more dramatic way than you might have ever imagined.

I have been pondering this idea for decades. Sometimes it was triggered by a conversation with a faith-minded leader who opted out of tired, conventional faith-work constructs because of their lack of real-world helpfulness. Sometimes a personal work challenge kicked me back to this question. And sometimes it was triggered by an encounter with a particular passage of Scripture.

Let me share a slice of biblical narrative that captured my curiosity years ago and has never left me. It was the primary inspiration for *The Gospel Goes to Work*.

THE GOSPEL UNIVERSAL AND PARTICULARIZED

Doctor Luke tells the story of the rustic preacher John down by the Jordan River reacting to the crowds coming to him for baptism. Suddenly, these words exploded from John's mouth:

Brood of snakes! What do you think you're doing slithering down here to the river? Do you think a little water on your snakeskins is going to deflect God's judgment?[2]

Apparently John had not taken any classes in how to win friends, influence people, and boost social media likes.

He went on thundering at the fresh converts,

It's your life that must change, not your skin. And don't think you can pull rank by claiming Abraham as "father." Being a child of Abraham is neither here nor there—children of Abraham are a dime a dozen. God can make children from stones if he wants. What counts is your life. Is it green and blossoming? Because if it's deadwood, it goes on the fire.

A change of life. Real repentance. Here was the gospel. It was a message that all John's listeners—young and old, male and female, rich and poor, rural and urban, workers of all types—

needed to hear. It was a universal invitation that still applies across the board centuries later. In other words, here's the baseline. A basic message to all humanity.

But notice what happened next: at the end of his sermon people started raising their hands with questions.

Now, my guess is that John felt good about his sermon. It had lots of volume, quotes from the Old Testament, and even some colorful illustrations connected to real life. What could the people possibly have any questions about?

The crowd asked him, "Then what are we supposed to do?"

The crowds needed a more specific application. They needed a "take-home," as one of my pastors calls it. They were internalizing the message and needed an actionable item to go and do.

So John answered their universal question:

"If you have two coats, give one away," he said. "Do the same with your food."

This should have applied to almost everyone in the crowd that day. The idea of taking care of those less fortunate was a part of their tradition and heritage. Those who had more should share with those who had less. That is what I call the baseline. He offered a starting point or universal minimum for all listeners regardless of their personality, title, age, background, and other particulars. Baseline established!

Extended sermon over. Everyone should be clear and ready to depart now. But then another subset of the group shouts out a question. And notice that this subset is a particular work group.

Tax men also came to be baptized and said, "Teacher, what should we do?"

Now, here is where we cannot miss the lane change. A particular group needed the message to be specifically shaped for their industry. John had already delivered a full bucket of truth and had even given the extended sermon where he broke down a personal application for his whole audience. But evidently that was not good enough. The tax collectors wanted a more customized application of the gospel message for their own career field.

So John told them, "No more extortion—collect only what is required by law."

This answer was dead-on. Everyone knew that a tax collector had a sliding scale of collections. He must give Caesar his portion, but he could also bully people into paying more. Everything extra was his personal bonus system. That is how he funded his new room addition, the college classes at Jerusalem University, and a beach vacation on the Mediterranean. And there was no ceiling to what he could collect.

Notice John did not just say, "Be honest and fair." Instead, he told the people what honesty and fairness looked like in the work setting of every tax collector. And did you catch that no one followed up, asking for an explanation? They immediately knew it to be true. The blue-sky concept begins to emerge as the tax collectors personalized the truth and insight.

Second extended sermon over. Time to break and get a few baptisms done. Then lunch. But another inquiry is heard above the chatter.

Soldiers asked him, "And what should we do?"

The obvious question we should be asking is, why can't the soldiers just do one of the two great applications John had already rolled out?

Because they were soldiers!

He told them, "No shakedowns, no blackmail—and be content with your rations."

Every soldier of Rome had clout. The uniform carried the power and authority of Caesar. And when they knocked on the door and accused you, the jury was already in. They had the freedom to claim anything they wanted, and your only response was "How much?" How much will it cost our family to keep Dad out of jail? What a dirty abuse of power and authority!

In this Q&A session we see the gospel going to work in different ways in different workplaces. For tax collectors, it was one thing. For soldiers, another. And we can be sure that the gospel applied in specific ways to fishermen, homemakers, woodworkers, scribes, and all other kinds of workers as well. There was a blue sky for each worker and each workplace to explore and apply the gospel message.

It's not that John was saying the gospel changes. It's that he knew the gospel has to be applied and nuanced for the particulars of a job. Kudos to Preacher John for not being unsettled by the questions and for knowing the specific answer to give each sector. (This should be a test given to every seminary graduate prior to handing over the degree.)

In the first application to share their goods, John illustrated the idea of the gospel baseline. In the two personalized applications to the soldiers and tax collectors, he opened up the idea of the gospel blue sky.

THE GOSPEL GOES TO WORK GRID

Baseline and blue sky—are you starting to see how this distinction will help you address the gospel fundamentals at work? You won't get a chance to forget those terms, because we're going to be returning to them throughout the rest of this book.

But there is one other framework to understand if you are going to grasp the message of this book. The gospel conversation can either be about me or about my company. Or as I will say, the gospel has both an *individual* and an *organization* application.

When you merge the baseline/blue sky pair with the individual/organizational pair, you get *The Gospel Goes to Work Grid.* It covers the whole range of workplace expressions of the gospel. With this grid, you can help to fill in the empty spaces of life's canvas with gospel paint.

Let me share my opinion right out of the gate: I believe the vast majority of writings and sermons have been locked into the bottom left quadrant and yet the greatest region for kingdom exploration is the top right quadrant. One of the reasons most of the dialogue has been around the individual baseline is because that is where pastors and theologians are most comfortable and respected. Therefore, it often takes someone coming out of the commercial markets or from the street to create more specific dialogue and application in the workplace. I have held a conviction for years that the practitioners in the workforce are the experts when it comes to application and expression of the gospel going to work. They know the most and have the best stories when it comes to gospel application. But generally, they are head

INDIVIDUAL BLUE SKY	ORGANIZATIONAL BLUE SKY
INDIVIDUAL BASELINE Chapter 5	ORGANIZATIONAL BASELINE

down doing work every day and not out crusading thought life and pedagogy. Hence, we often simply recycle the same information around the bottom left quadrant.

In the four chapters to follow, we'll be going in depth into each quadrant of the grid. You're going to see how all this applies to you and your workplace, and I think you'll be excited about the ideas it sparks in your mind. Right now, though, I want to give you a quick preview of each quadrant. Consider this a sampler plate to whet your appetite.

THE BASELINE FOR THE INDIVIDUAL.

Here's a question you may never have considered: What are the things that every follower of Jesus, regardless of their skills and temperament, their work setting, and the kind of work they perform, can do to represent Jesus well?

You might wonder, *Is it even possible to come up with a list that will encompass the CEO and the factory line worker, people in publicly owned corporations and owners of mom-and-pop shops, manual laborers and office denizens?*

I believe it *is* possible. In fact, I'd like to introduce four things every worker can do regardless of their personality, setting, or kind of work:

1. Evidence calling.
2. Display character.
3. Deliver skill.
4. Model serving.

Some of these are actions that most people of faith would agree that they should exhibit. Some of them might be more surprising or need additional explanation. Yet I believe that all of these are not only possible but necessary in establishing the gospel threshold for any worker doing any work in any kind of work setting.

THE BLUE SKY FOR THE INDIVIDUAL

At the risk of sounding obvious, I want to point out something: *people are different.* Even two people working at the same kind of job in the same company can be strikingly different in their personalities, interests, gifts, passions, and ambitions. So even if both of them were followers of Christ, they wouldn't naturally express the gospel in the same way.

A Christian who has the gift of helps, for example, might be the person in the office who organizes meal delivery for a fellow employee who has had a death in the family. A Christian with the wiring of a teacher may start an early morning Bible study for anyone who wants to come. And someone else will engage in the company's mercy and justice efforts. It's all about discovering the gospel expressions tied to our particular God-given wiring, not just spiritual gifts but also temperament, talents, and passions.

I can't give you a list for what your gospel blue-sky actions or attitudes on the job will look like, as I can with the baseline approach. That's because everyone's blue-sky list is different. But if you've got a holy ambition burning inside you for people to know and honor God, then I have no doubt that you will be able to think of some ideas for how to approach your career differently.

When we get to Chapter 6, I'll give you a lot more help to dream up ways of projecting the gospel through your own personality into your patch of blue sky.

THE BASELINE FOR THE ORGANIZATION

Think back to the Luke 3 passage about John the Baptist and the "snakes." I want to point out something you may not have noticed: the individuals who asked questions of John the Baptist about how to contextualize the gospel are not individually named. They are referred to as "tax men" and "soldiers." It's as if the focus is on these inquirers as representatives of their professions.

Gospel influence is not just for individual workers. It's for their organizations and entire industries too.

But is there a universal baseline for all organizations and every company in any industry? In other words, are there certain thresholds that any organization doing any kind of work should embody if it hopes to be a gospel carrier? I think so. These make up the organizational baseline:

1. A multiple bottom line
2. A culture of grace and truth
3. A stewardship motivation
4. Humble collaboration
5. Humane treatment of people

When I describe these five qualities, you may think I'm only talking about "Christian organizations"—ministries and churches. But that's not the case. Most of these characteristics can define the baseline of all kinds of organizations in the business and social sectors.

You may also think that the only people who can instill these values in an organization are the top bosses. That is not necessarily true either. Any lower-level workers can advocate for these values and model them in their own part of the organization. I'll be explaining more about how to do that in Chapter 7.

THE BLUE SKY FOR THE ORGANIZATION

Obviously, some types of organizations are more faith centric in their culture, products, and services. But *any* type of organization can head toward the gospel blue sky if one or more of the leaders is trying to get it there. The organization may never use a Bible verse or sell a "Christian" product or service, but it can still contribute to God's renewal process in an extraordinary way by how it operates.

What does it look like for a theater company to be informed and shaped by the gospel? For a bank? For a classical academy? For a digital media company? For a congressional lobbying firm? For a global manufacturer or retailer?

I don't know exactly. But the followers of Jesus inside all of these organizations and more can figure it out. And the world will be gospelized when organizations large and small, and of all types, ask the kinds of questions posed to John the Baptist two thousand years ago. This is both the most overlooked and the most important quadrant of the grid.

WHAT ABOUT NONBELIEVERS?

As we consider how the gospel displays itself in the four quadrants of the grid, sooner or later we are likely to ask ourselves, *Can only a Christian worker or a faith-based organization reflect the gospel?* The answer is no, and what's really interesting is that this answer drives us back to the source of gospel power.

If you'll recall from the Bible, Jesus commended the parental devotion of a Syro-Phoenician woman. He respected the repentance of the Ninevites in Jonah's day. He was amazed by the faith of a Roman centurion. He highlighted the gratitude of a Samaritan.[3] It seems undeniable, then, that people who are not followers of Jesus are capable of doing good.

"PEOPLE WHO HAVE BEEN
TRANSFORMED BY FAITH
HAVE A DIFFERENT LEVEL OF
INTIMACY, INTENTIONALITY,
AND ENGAGEMENT WITH THE
GOSPEL THAN PEOPLE WHO
DO NOT HAVE FAITH."

We know this from personal experience. People of no faith, or of a different faith, often behave honorably at work. They can labor hard to make the most of the skill they have. They can be honest. They can be wise leaders, generous servants, and fair negotiators.

In fact, I would go so far as to say that people of no faith often put Jesus followers to shame through the ways they let gospel values shine at work on a baseline level. Many times, for example, they are better at establishing a respectful culture among co-workers, more energetic in pursuing sustainable business practices, or more active in using organizational resources for community programs than we are.

How can that be?

It goes back to what we have in common—we were all created in the image of God. Even those without faith, then, can in part reflect a gospel hot spot through their nature as image bearers of God. This means that ultimately it is God who deserves the credit for the good that nonbelievers do. We should be eager to recognize His work through people who are atheists or non-Christians.

Here is the single differentiator—pure faith. As my buddy Bill says, faith in Jesus introduces the supernatural element. People who have been transformed by faith have a different level of intimacy, intentionality, and engagement with the gospel than people who do not have faith. We have a power source outside ourselves, motivating us to activate the gospel in the world. The gospel is the life-giving agenda of God.

I bet I've read Luther's famous quote on the demolition of the faith/work divide a hundred times. But every time I read it, my heart is stabbed again by the single leveling differentiator of all work, workers, and work settings. It is my faith. "The works of monks and priests, however arduous they be," Luther said, "do not differ one whit in the sight of God from the works of the rustic laborer in the field, but that all works are measured by faith alone."[4]

God gives the gospel its power, whether He is working through Christians or non-Christians.

Think about it: What can I learn from non-Christians in the business world about doing good for humanity?

THE STAR OF THE SHOW

Whether we're talking about gospel-friendly practices down at the baseline level or those up in the blue sky, there's something we need to remember: Primarily, this isn't about what we do for God. It's about what God is already doing and invites us to participate in with Him. Hudson Taylor, the pioneer missionary who spent fifty-one years in China, said it this way, "I used to ask God to help me. Then I asked if I might help Him. I ended up by asking God to do His work through me."[5]

God is already at work, renewing all things and reconciling the whole world to Himself. The most important leader among us is never anything more than a bit player in the gospel drama. That isn't to demean our role; it is to free us from an unnecessary burden. And at the same time, it will help us to see what a shame it would be if we didn't join in such a great work that is winding its way to consummation through the millennia of human history.

I hope you'll approach the gospel baseline as a discipline to pursue. And I hope you'll dream and scheme for the gospel blue sky. But as you do so, seek the wisdom and the guidance of God. Because He is already there ahead of you.

"I USED TO ASK GOD TO
HELP ME. THEN I ASKED IF
I MIGHT HELP HIM. I ENDED
UP BY ASKING GOD TO DO HIS
WORK THROUGH ME."
—HUDSON TAYLOR

CHAPTER 5

A PURPOSE-DRIVEN JOB

"A cobbler, a smith, a farmer, each has the work and office of his trade, and yet they are all alike consecrated priests and bishops, and every one by mean of his own work or office must benefit and serve every other."[1]
—Martin Luther, An Open Letter to the Christian Nobility

MOST OF US look in the rearview mirror at our career so far and have a few smiles at things that went well, a few frowns at the opposite kind of outcomes, and a few quizzical expressions because we still don't understand what happened. One of my biggest smiles was the launching and publishing of a magazine called *Life@Work* during the late 1990s and early 2000s. My partners in this publishing enterprise were my friends Tom and Sean. Our magazine won awards in every category as we rode a rocket of growth until the year we sold it.

I often tell my clients, "Everyone loves to jump on a rocket." In other words, if your company or work has lots of upward pull, then opportunities abound on that trajectory. And that's exactly what happened for us as a result of the success of *Life@Work*.

Tom and I had been assisting the board of the men's ministry Promise Keepers (newly created at the time) with their strategy and direction. Now the leaders of PK asked us to speak at some of the ministry's mega stadium events. I don't mind telling you that, for me, standing in front of eighty thousand men at the first event where I was scheduled to speak (in the old Detroit Silverdome) was a bit overwhelming. But I wanted the men to see that, through their work, they could be a part of God's plan. I wanted them to adopt the belief that God's canvas of calling and renewal was big and wide and could include every single one of the eighty thousand

INDIVIDUAL BLUE SKY	ORGANIZATIONAL BLUE SKY
INDIVIDUAL BASELINE Chapter 5	ORGANIZATIONAL BASELINE

men! I wanted them to see that they did not have to quit their jobs and join a church staff to be on God's first team for kingdom impact and service.

We built our talk around a question: *What is the minimum standard or lowest common denominator for taking your faith to work?* Sound familiar? That's the individual baseline I introduced in the last chapter. We wanted to address every man doing any kind of work, in any kind of work setting, for the largest purpose. We were looking for a guideline that could be applied to every face and all listeners.

We found our answer in Psalm 78:70-72:

> *He chose David his servant*
> *and took him from the sheep pens;*
> *from tending the sheep he brought him*
> *to be the shepherd of his people Jacob,*
> *of Israel his inheritance.*
> *And David shepherded them with integrity of heart;*
> *with skillful hands he led them.*

This little passage reveals four key baseline benchmarks for the gospel going to work:

+ "He chose David"—*calling*
+ "David his servant"—*service*
+ "Shepherded them with integrity of heart"—*character*
+ "With skillful hands he led them"—*skill*

To be clear, these are not qualities that only certain kinds of people can hope to possess. They are universal. They apply to both men and women, to executives and hourly workers, to the shy and the gregarious, and to younger and older workers alike.

The need to know what it looks like, at a minimum, to represent the gospel well at work is just as great now as it was back in 1998 when I spoke at the Promise Keepers mega-events. And in fact, I believe that today there is a resurgence of interest in this subject. It's time to pick the message back up.[2]

I consider the four qualities from Psalm 78 to be foundation stones that, when mortared together, make up the foundation for the individual who wants to go to work with the gospel.

FOUNDATION STONE 1: YOU GIVE EVIDENCE OF YOUR CALLING.

I remember standing in front of a sea of faces at the Promise Keepers event held in the old Texas Stadium, near Dallas, and proclaiming to the crowd, "I feel called to be a businessman." The large sporting event stadium grew unusually quiet. I could sense the men considering the idea that their jobs could be a divine vocation.

Let me ask: Why do you do *your* work? Is it only because you need the money? Are you just putting in time until you can find something better to do or until you retire? Regi Campbell says, "The primary objective for most people's career is to eliminate the need for it."[3]

Or do you see your work as something anchored to God's call and gifting of you? Are there divine assignments and a divine audience attached to your work? Or do you really think those concepts only ride along with professional ministry work?

Is yours just a job or an energized vocation?

Are you employed or are you called?

I'm not trying to downplay the problems or disappointments you might face in your work. Maybe you're dealing with repetitive tasks, low morale, equally low pay, a lousy boss, an employee revolt, or missed sales targets. But I *am* saying that, despite whatever problems you might face, God still has a divine agenda for you and your work. As Nietzsche observed, "He who has a why to live for can bear almost any how."[4] And your calling is the why.

The difference between career and calling is the difference between mission and activity. Calling is being released to be exactly who I am supposed to be, to do precisely what I am supposed to do for God: an assignment with enduring worth.

Os Guinness said, "Calling is the Archimedean point by which faith moves the world."[5] Work can have eternal purpose, and our lives can have fullness of meaning through the work we do.

What more compelling reason to get up when the alarm sounds each morning than knowing that God has assigned your work and cares about its quality? What a motivation! A calling provides the perfect antidote to our self-serving, self-consuming view of work. With a sense of calling in our day-to-day work, we are leveraged in eternity, settled in deep fulfillment.

People of faith who express calling in their work stick out—there is evidence of faith and divine leading everywhere they turn.

First, let others know that you have a calling by how you act about your job. Show up for work fully engaged—mind, body, heart, and soul. In a work world where so many are trying to get by while doing the minimum, throwing yourself wholly into your work will let people know that work means something different for you. In this way, you can evidence your calling without saying one word about it.

"BRING YOUR HEAD AND YOUR
HEART TO WORK EVERY DAY.
DON'T JUST GO THROUGH
THE MOTIONS."

Bring your head and your heart to work every day. Don't just go through the motions. Until we do that, there is no reason to use religious language about how we see and approach our work.

But it starts with a real epiphany of sorts. I am called or summoned to my work every day. My big payday is well down the road, when my Creator renders His reward on my life and work.

FOUNDATION STONE 2: YOU DISPLAY CHARACTER ON THE JOB.

The word for "character" in the New Testament comes from a Greek term describing an engraving instrument. The picture is of an artist who wears a groove on a metal plate by repeatedly etching the same place with a sharp tool. After repeated strokes, an image takes shape.

My character is forged as a set of distinctive marks that, together, illustrate a portrait of who I really am. Everyone has character. But the *quality of character* can be described: bad or good, shifty or sturdy, sordid or sterling.

Behavior and character are related, but they are not the same thing. Behavior is *what I do*. Character is *the person my behavior has built*. Behavior is just one action—"I behaved badly in that situation." Character is the sum of my behaviors, public and private, arranged consistently across the spectrum of my life. Any behavior, duplicated and reduplicated, forms a part of my character.

Every time we make a decision, we cut a groove. Every time we react to a crisis, we cut a groove. When we hold our tongues and practice self-control, or when we let them run loose and speak our minds, we are carving our character. When we say yes or no to a reckless temptation, we are signing our names. When you stand up to peer pressure, hold the line on truth, or return kindness for cruelty, you are cutting the pattern of your character.

There's no overnight delivery on character. You build it up gradually over time. Then it comes into play when it's needed. My character becomes the connective thread of my "eulogy virtues regardless what my résumé virtues" are, as David Brooks says in his thoughtful book *The Road to Character*.[6]

The boss who has developed a habit of caring for people will treat his employees as human beings who have feelings, not as tools to accomplish his will.

The marketing director who values honesty will practice truth in advertising and not over-hype her company's offerings.

The team lead that is striving for humility will resist the temptation to take credit for an idea someone else put forth first.

If we're developing godly character, we'll make sure our résumé tells the strict truth. We'll under-promise and over-deliver, instead of the other way around. We won't overstate earnings to make investors happy. We won't instruct customer service to cover up mistakes in order to hold on to clients. We won't call in sick when the truth is that we just don't feel like working that day. We'll handle our company's money and physical assets with scrupulous integrity.

No amount of business ethics training has been able to establish consistent integrity in the workplace. But habits engraved over time because of a faith motivation can turn the way we do business into a slight reflection of the flawless character of God.

FOUNDATION STONE 3: YOU DELIVER SKILL CONSISTENTLY.

I've observed something that's disturbing to me: Often, when faith goes up, skill goes down. In other words, when people become more involved in their faith journey, they sometimes become less valuable at work. I don't know for sure why this is. Maybe it's because, to people in this situation, performance on the job seems less important in comparison with spiritual pursuits. Maybe their minds and hearts are occupied elsewhere. But in any case, they're not delivering the devotion and ability to their work that they used to. The boss might go to them if he wants somebody to pray about a crisis in his family, but if he needs somebody to close a deal or figure out a strategic problem, he'll go to somebody else.

This is the opposite of the gospel going to work. It's the gospel going on extended vacation, and it's wrong. Dorothy Sayers, the late English essayist and poet, remarked, "The Church's approach to an intelligent carpenter is usually to exhort him not to be drunk and disorderly in his leisure hours, and to come to church on Sundays. What the Church should be telling him is this: that the very first demand that his religion makes upon him is that he should make very good tables."[7]

Scripture challenges followers of Christ to raise the bar in their work, not lower the curve. Consider the parable of the talents.

When many people look at this parable by Jesus, they begin to focus on the concept of stewardship—what we do with God's gifts to us. But before we go there, we should look at how the parable starts out, the set-up:

"THE CHURCH'S APPROACH TO AN INTELLIGENT CARPENTER IS USUALLY TO EXHORT HIM NOT TO BE DRUNK AND DISORDERLY IN HIS LEISURE HOURS, AND TO COME TO CHURCH ON SUNDAYS. WHAT THE CHURCH SHOULD BE TELLING HIM IS THIS: THAT THE VERY FIRST DEMAND THAT HIS RELIGION MAKES UPON HIM IS THAT HE SHOULD MAKE VERY GOOD TABLES."

–DOROTHY SAYERS

[The kingdom of heaven] will be like a man going on a journey, who called his servants and entrusted his wealth to them. To one he gave five bags of gold, to another two bags, and to another one bag, each according to his ability. Then he went on his journey.[8]

In this parable, the man going on the journey represents God, and the bags of gold represent the abilities and opportunities God gives us. In other words, God passes out skill sets to all of us. So a part of our purpose in life is to discover our inborn greatness by figuring out what our skill sets are. Then we can learn to utilize those skills to the utmost in every sphere of life, including work. We just can't give in to the tendency to get sloppy or lackadaisical on the job.

Delivering skill matters to God because He is the epitome of skillfulness. In His creation, in His moral law, in the redemptive plan He is carrying out, He is perfect and effective in all He does. He excels at every good thing. He is simply the best there is, the archetype of skill.

And let's not forget that He made us in His image. This means we have a capacity to voluntarily appreciate and imitate God's excellence. He gave us the ability to choose to do our best. Our work becomes worship when we willfully give of our best every day for the good of those around us through our jobs.

God created skill to be a mastery that is, at its heart, constructive and creative. It is the weapon, not of unhealthy competition, but of commitment to the welfare of others. Here's what that looks like:

+ A mechanic finds and fixes a problem that no one else could locate, much less solve.
+ An entrepreneur creates a successful business from nothing.

- A professional truck driver maneuvers an eighteen-wheeler into a dock with only inches of leeway on either side.
- A tenacious salesman negotiates through almost insurmountable obstacles to close a deal.
- An artist brings living color out of a blank white canvas.
- A writer arranges words to make a reader's blood boil, the heart laugh, or the mind reflect.

Booker T. Washington observed, "Excellence is to do a common thing in an uncommon way."[9] So even if our work has begun to seem ordinary or boring to us, we can learn to bring our best to it and carry it off with excellence. As we do so, we will be imitating our heavenly Father and bringing Him pleasure. We'll also be making gospel life bloom in our workplace.

FOUNDATION STONE 4: YOU MODEL SERVICE TO OTHERS.

Regardless of our occupation, our title, and our authority, if we work around people, we can model serving. Serving is not a function of status, power, or station. Leaders ought to serve. Executives ought to serve. Presidents ought to serve.

Serving is simply having the energy and focus for others that we always end up finding for ourselves. Any and all of us can serve.

- It means coming in early or staying late to help a co-worker who is staring down a deadline and needs help.
- It means discovering what your co-workers' aspirations are and actually spending some energy to help them achieve that.
- It means becoming a good listener, not just a good talker.

- It means taking the time to figure out how I can affirm someone else, get someone else promoted, get someone else's project funded, not just my own.
- It means having someone's back when they are not present to defend themselves.

Any of us can do that. It is not a question of IQ, education, training, or even job experience. Serving does not even require a job interview. You see a need and meet it—it's that simple.

Is serving risky? Yes, it is. People are messy. The closer you get to them, the higher your chances of getting dirty. Your service will not always be noticed or appreciated. It will often be taken for granted. It will drain you. Serving is literally spending yourself on behalf of others.

People hurt, people have emotions, people need direction, and people need leadership. Yet in the process of serving them, we will be stretched. Investing in others, we are enriched. As Bob Moawad suggests, "Help others get ahead. You will always stand taller with someone else on your shoulders."[10]

How do we know if we are serving others? Robert Greenleaf, in his book *On Becoming a Servant-Leader*, takes a look from the other side of serving. He suggests that we ask, "Do those being served grow as persons: do they, while being served, become healthier, wiser, freer, more autonomous, more likely themselves to become servants?"[11] Real service always grows others. Its bottom line must be measured in the lives of those around me.

Jesus modeled serving to His disciples by washing their feet. Serving has a way of leading to more serving. By making ourselves lowly as servants, we may be setting off a chain reaction that winds up elevating everyone around us. And when that happens, the gospel goes with us to work.

Think about it: Would your co-workers say you have interest and energy in their world or would they write you off as only self-serving?

POWERFUL IF PRACTICED

These foundation stones, if practiced, are powerful:

> *Give evidence of your calling.*
> *Display character.*
> *Deliver skill.*
> *Model serving.*

And they're all within your reach. You don't need to delay, debate, or ask anyone's permission. You just need to do them.

Now I want to give you a warning and an encouragement. First, the warning:

Don't try to leap over the baseline. You have to start here.

We all want to be exceptional. The gospel has meant so much to us that we want to do amazing things to live it out for others. If we're ambitious about our work in general, we're doubly ambitious with a gospel baseline.

If you neglect the baseline, you'll be hindering the gospel. It's what Jesus referred to as putting a basket over your lamp or letting your salt lose its flavor.[12] When that happens, there is no authentic starting point for the gospel in us. So we have to shore up our gospel living in these fundamental areas before building from there.

I think you get that.

And now I want to share the encouragement. The gospel baseline—even without venturing into the blue sky—is incredibly powerful. Don't underestimate it.

Try a mental exercise with me.

Imagine that you and every other follower of Jesus in your town or city spent the next year consistently living up to the four benchmarks of the individual baseline. For one year, you and the other people of faith gave evidence of your divine calling to your work. For one year, you and the others displayed the godly character engraved in you over time. For one year, you and the others delivered your God-given skill at your place of work with excellence and consistency. For one year, you and the others modeled serving—having as much energy for those around you as you do for yourself.

What do you think would be the result?

I'll tell you what I think would happen: I think it would raise the water level of the gospel in your community to flood stage. I think it would initiate a gospel movement reminiscent of some of the great revivals of past ages. It would flow out of the banks of the church and into the streets and through every channel of life and community. No corner of your community would be removed from the light, the salt, and the sweet aroma of the gospel. The churches in your community would grow at a rate they could not imagine. And the birthmarks of the gospel would begin to show up: mercy and justice, caring for the poor, being generous, treating others kindly, new converts to the good news story, revitalized old heads who had grown cold and calloused in their faith journey, and more.

Do your part in living out the baseline and see what happens. It might be the start of something big!

"THE DIFFERENCE BETWEEN
CAREER AND CALLING IS
THE DIFFERENCE BETWEEN
MISSION AND ACTIVITY."

CHAPTER 6

GOSPEL ENTREPRENEURSHIP

"For Christian faith not to be idle in the world, the work of doctors and garbage collectors, business executives and artists, stay-at-home moms or dads and scientists needs to be inserted into God's story with the world. That story needs to provide the most basic rules by which the game in all these spheres is played."[1]
—*Miroslav Volf*

THE SKY WASN'T literally blue on December 17, 1903, at Kitty Hawk, North Carolina—it was actually pretty hazy. But Wilbur and Orville Wright proved themselves to be blue-sky thinkers of the first order when they completed the first powered flight in history.

Behind them—millennia of humankind's sputtering attempts to soar through the air like the birds.

Before them—air mail, crop dusting, Charles Lindbergh, aircraft carriers, the boom that the sound barrier makes when it is broken, Apollo 11, the Space Shuttle, the Stealth fighter, and nano-drones (not to mention millions of little packages of airline peanuts).

The two brothers from Ohio were men who could dream the unachieved and were willing to work to make it a reality.

The business world has known many other blue-sky thinkers.

People like Steve Jobs and Steve Wozniak, who built computers in a garage and founded a company called Apple.

People like Larry Page, who imagined a search engine called Google that has become one of the most powerful companies on the planet.

People like Oprah Winfrey, who turned a personal career into a new way of reaching mega audiences and marketing content.

INDIVIDUAL
BLUE SKY
Chapter 6

ORGANIZATIONAL
BLUE SKY

INDIVIDUAL
BASELINE

ORGANIZATIONAL
BASELINE

In the last chapter we looked at the individual baseline—the starting place for all gospel expression in the workplace. Baseline compliance to the gospel as individuals is necessary and can be transformative even if that's all we do. Yet, there is more. Now we are looking at the individual blue sky—that region of a person's work world that invites godly ambition and healthy curiosity. That region where a worker taps into his or her own wiring and calling to harness the power, reach, and intent of the gospel.

I want you to think about the unique opportunities you have to practice the gospel in your particular work in your particular style. It may not be anything grandiose or dramatic, but it can be powerful and life-giving in its own way.

WEAR WHAT FITS

When young David volunteered for a showdown with the towering foreigner who had all of Israel's soldiers spooked, the king of Israel, Saul, offered to help him out. I imagine their conversation going something like this…

> SAUL: Kid, I can't believe you're actually going to go up against this giant, but if you're determined, the least I can do is give you some protection. Here, put on my armor. It's the best in the whole country.
>
> DAVID: Well, um, okay, worth a try, Your Highness.
>
> (Much clinking as David puts on armor that's unfamiliar and too large for him, then walks around trying it out)
>
> (Snickering from watching guards as David presents an awkward spectacle in the ill-fitting armor)

DAVID: Thanks anyway, King, but I'd better not use this armor when I go up against Goliath. I don't have any experience fighting in armor like this. I think I'd better stick with what I'm used to using out in the fields with my father's sheep.

Wisely, David took off the armor that was made for another and proceeded to select some smooth river stones for his sling—the weapons he had used to slay the bears and lions that tried to eat his father's sheep. We know what he did to the giant Goliath with them.[2]

"The point?" you ask.

Like him, we should reject conventional approaches to living out the gospel at work that might be fine for others but don't fit us. We must find the style that fits our unique, God-given wiring and faith narrative. And when we find it, we must face the daily giants with confidence and boldness.

The fact is, no two Jacks are the same and no two Jills are the same. No two jobs are identical. And no two workers on the job, even if they are doing similar work, are perfect duplicates. This is why we must personalize or customize the gospel application based upon who we are, what kind of work we're doing, and the setting within which we do our work.

Only when you are making your own unique contribution to the gospel in the world of work will you be able to give God the greatest glory of which you are capable. Only when you are singing with your own voice and wearing your own wardrobe will you find fulfillment. If you're mimicking someone else, or role-playing, like so many others, you won't likely honor God much. But as you operate in your best skill set, you will have your maximum impact on the world and will generate maximum glory for God.

"ONLY WHEN YOU
ARE SINGING WITH
YOUR OWN VOICE AND
WEARING YOUR OWN
WARDROBE WILL YOU
FIND FULFILLMENT.
IF YOU'RE MIMICKING
SOMEONE ELSE, OR
ROLE-PLAYING, LIKE
SO MANY OTHERS, YOU
WON'T LIKELY HONOR
GOD MUCH."

Remember the story of John the Baptist applying the gospel to soldiers and tax collectors? This is what we're doing now—figuring out how to maximize the gospel in our particular jobs and professions. As daunting as it might be, we need to explore the individual blue sky to find the ultimate energy and impact intended with our lives.

KNOW THYSELF, EXPRESS THYSELF

One key to figuring out the best way for *you* to apply the gospel into the blue sky goes back to one of the oldest and most enduring pieces of advice that human history has for us:

Know thyself.

What are the variables that make you, *you*, and that make your work, *your work*, and that therefore make certain types of gospel expression on the job more appropriate and liberating for *you*? There are many variables, but I want to focus on four that have proved themselves over and over to be crucial. As you read about these four variables, think about how they help to differentiate you from others, framing your unique expression of gospel translation to the world around you.

1. GENERATION

It's possible to make too much of the generations and start indulging in unwarranted "generationalizing." But I believe there's validity to the idea that the time when you were born and the cohort you grew up with can have a shaping effect on you. That's true with how you work. It's also true with how you take the gospel to work.

Picture Susan and Karen. Both are nurses working in the same medical group. Both are natural-born people helpers. Both are Christians who want to represent the gospel faithfully. But Susan is 60 and Karen is 25. Are they going to represent the gospel at work in the same exact way? I'd be surprised if they did.

As an aging Baby Boomer, Susan is likely to be more tied to church-based activities and probably more disposed to the traditional spiritual disciplines and exercises. She might be likely to invite someone to a church service or a women's Bible study.

As a Millennial, Karen is likely to be more integrated in the way she sees and expresses doing good and sowing kingdom seeds. She might be less overt in her language of the gospel and be way more comfortable with the "outsiders" than Susan.

Of the three generations that make up nearly the whole of today's workforce—Boomers, Xers, and Millennials—the largest is the Millennials. It is also the group that is going to have the greatest impact on the workplace over the next decade or more. So the approach that Millennial Christians take to the gospel is especially worth watching.

When I asked my friend Dave Blanchard of Praxis about Millennials taking their faith to work, he argued that the members of his cause-oriented generation are natives to good works. Yet they can also face dilemmas. Dave said,

> For the Millennials, work is not work so much as it is "What am I going to do with my life?" The idea that faith wouldn't be relevant to work seems odd; it's only a matter of whether others "get it." Social ventures are now the hottest places to work. TOMS, Warby Parker, Invisible Children, and charity:water trump even Nike and World Vision. To channel Alex Bogusky, faith and work is now "baked in" to the brand.

This discussion isn't always about whether a particular generation is living out the gospel "right" or "wrong." It's also about recognizing how your age-cohort perspective—whatever it is—might make certain kinds of gospel expressions more natural or suitable for you. Stick with the effective approaches and don't worry about adopting others that might come more easily to people of a different generation.

Knowing the characteristics of your generation can provide valuable clues to shaping your blue-sky gospel strategy.

2. PERSONAL WIRING

We're *all* made in God's image, but beautifully crafted as a one-of-a-kind creation. That's why Mike and Michelle, two Christians working in software development at Google, will flow the gospel differently. That's why Beth and Ben, two Christians working in shops on Main Street of the same small town, will likewise take the gospel to work differently.

As a part of His individualizing creation, God gave us different spiritual gifts. The apostle Paul named more than a dozen spiritual gifts, and even these probably do not represent an exhaustive listing.[3]

Our spiritual gifts have a direct bearing on how we reflect the gospel at work. Someone with the gift of exhortation might be an agitator to get her company started on sustainability practices. Someone with the gift of mercy might want to join in a community outreach program for disadvantaged children.

In addition to spiritual gifts, God also gave us different personalities. How many personality types are there? There's no agreement on this either. The Big Five theory of personality looks at (obviously) five types. The Enneagram highlights nine. The popular Myers-Briggs model gives acronyms to sixteen personality profiles.

My three children are all grown now, but when each of

"WE'RE ALL MADE IN
GOD'S IMAGE, BUT
BEAUTIFULLY CRAFTED
AS A ONE-OF-A-KIND
CREATION."

them was in high school, my wife and I took them to see our friend Robyn, who does personality inventory testing. We knew that, even though our kids were siblings who had grown up in the same house, each one had unique wiring. We wanted them to know their personalities and start using that information as they began looking ahead toward their careers and the rest of their lives.

In the same way, we all should evaluate our own personality tendencies to think about how we could express the gospel best. If you're a Myers-Briggs INFJ, you might want to plan a community service project for your company. If you're an ESFP, you'll likely prefer offering support to people on a one-on-one basis.

Apart from spiritual gifts and personality, what talents do you have? What types of service get you excited? Pay attention to your individual traits and passions. Your unique wiring is a distinguishing quality of how you might nuance the gospel application. Throw off the traditional garb and pick up the tools that are central to your style and created greatness.

3. FAITH JOURNEY AND LIFE EXPERIENCES

Meet Mike, Julie, and Leon. Mike grew up a conservative Baptist in the South. Julie is a member of a Reformed church in Michigan. Leon, hailing from the Pacific Northwest, had no faith history until he met some believers at the local university.

These three all want to live out the gospel in their workplaces. But their respective religious backgrounds have equipped them to do it differently.

Or consider Dave, Anya, and Maria. Dave and his wife lost a child to leukemia, sending Dave into a long period of depression and doubt from which he is only now recovering. Anya was a prodigal and a rebel for many years, before repenting in dramatic fashion and getting fired up for Jesus. Maria has lived quietly and consistently as a part of the same faith community for her entire life.

When these three start mapping out their blue-sky strategies for having a gospel influence at work, how are their formative faith experiences going to influence them? They certainly won't all three go about it in the same way.

Some people have spent their Christian lives approaching their faith primarily as doers. Others as thinkers. Still others as feelers. Our base wiring will always be represented in the way we take the gospel to work.

A person who is a new believer may be filled with enthusiasm for outreach, which is great. But he or she might need some mentoring or partnership with someone more mature in the faith to know how to effectively go about spreading the gospel.

I've known people who have been the subjects of spiritual abuse to be effective in portraying the gospel authentically to people who are wary of anything connected to church. That's an example of how our unique experiences equip us to reflect the gospel.

I could go on and on with the variations on belief systems and faith-influencing experiences that set us apart from one another. These differences give us natural tendencies that can guide us as we dream about launching the gospel into the blue sky over our workplace.

4. WORK TYPE AND WORK SETTING

In his oral history *Working*, Studs Terkel recorded the voices of working men and women telling of their likes and dislikes, fears, problems, and happiness on the job.[4] One of the reminders his book gives is simply the sheer diversity of

"SOME PEOPLE HAVE
SPENT THEIR CHRISTIAN
LIVES APPROACHING
THEIR FAITH PRIMARILY
AS DOERS. OTHERS AS
THINKERS. STILL OTHERS
AS FEELERS. OUR BASE
WIRING WILL ALWAYS BE
REPRESENTED IN THE WAY
WE TAKE THE GOSPEL
TO WORK."

the kinds of work that people do. Studs interviewed people ranging from cleaning people to stockbrokers to farmers to athletes.

Even the Bible mentions dozens of types of jobs. Gideon was a farmer; Dorcas, a seamstress; Luke, a doctor; Daniel, a government official; Lydia, a commercial business woman—just to name a few. The Bible's jobs list includes armor bearers, brick makers, chariot driver, doorkeepers, treasurers, and watchmen. Today there isn't much of a call for armor bearers or chariot drivers, but on the other hand, we have a lot of new kinds of jobs that Moses, David, and Peter wouldn't have recognized.

Or think about the different categories of workplace: Large company and small company. Public and private. Start-up and mature company. Service oriented and product based. Local and global.

The same individual can go to work at Whole Foods corporate or at a boutique marketing firm that represents products from Africa going into retailers around the world. Those different workplaces offer different opportunities for contextualizing the gospel.

With an online article, Brian Dijkema reminded me of one particular area we tend to overlook when we think about the gospel being expressed in different work arenas: blue collar and less-skilled labor.[5] Dijkema says,

We get excited about those who open local coffee shops or become journalists or start a non-profit or (fill in the blank). But what do our "faith and work" books have to say to people who work on the line at a Ford assembly plant, or to medical assistants who take care of the elderly? Will landscapers and receptionists see themselves in the "work" we're talking about? Would anyone who has to wear coveralls to work feel comfortable at our "faith and work" conferences?

Although we don't always sufficiently recognize it, blue-collar jobs offer just as many opportunities for the gospel as white-collar jobs do. It's just that those opportunities are different. The blue sky is for the blue collar too. Any color collar (or for that matter, a dirty t-shirt with no collar) has a unique blue sky of gospel exploration at work.

A craftsman can glorify God by making beautiful things and then donate a percentage of profits to her college roommate doing a water project in Africa.

An actor can portray the complexity and richness of human relationships with a sense of realness that shows he is not removed from the humanity around us.

A football coach can find his unique voice and style to keep the kids both growing and winning.

A tenured professor can recreate new content every year for her sociology class because she is wired for content, and that freshness can set her apart from the stale reruns that many classes are made of.

A banker wired for encouragement can call people after their loan was declined and guide them on where to go and how to make the changes to get the loan next time or with someone else.

Again, the gospel can go to work with any worker doing any kind of work in any work setting. But *how* that happens can look beautifully diverse. Because our Creator is beautifully diverse and creative.

GOSPEL GAPS

Unlike our discussion of the individual baseline, I can't tell you exactly how to pursue a blue-sky approach to the gospel for your work and workplace. You're going to have to wrestle with that on your own. There's no easy or automated way to design your strategy. John the Baptist is not around for you to raise your hand and ask his advice.

But I do have one piece of advice that has worked for many: look for the "gospel gaps," as a friend calls them. In other words, look at your job, your team, and the work you're doing and identify where gospel values are not prevailing. Then pray and act toward injecting gospel goodness into those gaps. Where are the crevices of darkness into which the light could shine beauty and goodness? Where are the ugly, rotten deeds and behaviors to which the salt and sweet aroma of the gospel could bring redemption and renewal? Where is the corruption to which gospel leaven could bring irreversible change?

Remember that when John the Baptist replied to the tax collectors and the soldiers, he contextualized the gospel for problems in their lines of work. For the tax collectors—don't collect more taxes than you're supposed to. For the soldiers—don't extort money. These were gospel gaps in their respective professions.

In your line of work, where is there a lack of integrity? Where are corners being cut? Where are people and the environment being mistreated? Where are bad business practices being accepted because of laziness or mediocrity? What are the unexploited gospel opportunities? How might you glorify God in your work in a way that you are not currently doing? Where can you "tear a corner off of the darkness"—as Bono describes in his poetic style—and bring goodness to bear?[6] Figure out how you can fill these gaps with blue-sky gospel expression born out of who you are.

As you wrestle with calculations like these, let me assure you that it can bring you closer to God. It can actually be a part of your faith development.

Mike Duke has been a good friend for a long time. I

watched him move his way through the corporate world, eventually arriving at the CEO seat of one of the largest companies in the world (Walmart). Mike has never left his faith at home, on the shelf, or in the closet when going to work. But he has had to find his voice and style for greatest gospel effectiveness. Mike has used the power of story and symbols to convey his faith throughout his career. He has also used a gentle spirit of humility as his day-in-day-out style of leading. And as an educated engineer, the methodical process of listening before talking, not jumping to impulsive conclusions, and approaching problems in a systematic manner was perhaps easier and more natural to him. His individual faith expression in the blue sky required him to overlay his own calling, gifts, and style into each stop of his career.

It's easier to stay at the baseline, but when you set off like a rocket into the blue sky, it will kick your faith up to a new level. But to do that you must be yourself and let others be who they were created to be. Who knows what will happen then?

For the gospel to have its greatest possible effect, we need to have all kinds of people expressing it in all kinds of ways all over the place. In fact, the way I look at it is that effectiveness for the gospel is like brand impressions on social media.

GOSPEL IMPRESSIONS AND EXPRESSIONS

If you want to get your brand across on social media, you need lots of tweets and posts reaching plenty of fans and followers. In order to start marking an impact in the marketplace, you have to get the message out in all sorts of ways across as many platforms as possible. The many disparate impressions blend together to create a message imprint in the mind of the market.

Similarly, our culture needs many "gospel impressions" if it is going to close the gospel gaps. We need a broad diversity of individuals expressing the true gospel through their particular voice. There is more than one flavor of salt, more than one single color of light.

Christians often spend too much energy trying to make the salt of the gospel all the same flavor or dosage and overreach to standardize the light color and wattage. Sadly, this tendency to fit everyone into a one-size-fits-all box when it comes to representing the gospel is usually counterproductive on every front.

There is an individual baseline for all followers of Jesus to take the gospel to work—it is the bare essentials that when embraced will raise the gospel level in any workplace and community. And then there is an entire blue sky for individuals to find their gospel voice and practice gospel application in their particular work setting. As those things happen in concert, the reach, power, and intent of the gospel achieve their greatest extent.

"CHRISTIANS OFTEN
SPEND TOO MUCH ENERGY
TRYING TO MAKE THE
SALT OF THE GOSPEL ALL
THE SAME FLAVOR OR
DOSAGE AND OVERREACH TO
STANDARDIZE THE LIGHT
COLOR AND WATTAGE."

CHAPTER 7

EMBEDDING
THE GOSPEL

"We have somehow got hold of the idea that error is only that which is outrageously wrong and we do not seem to understand that the most dangerous person of all is the one who does not emphasize the right things."[1]
—Dr. Martyn Lloyd-Jones

THE HEALTH DEPARTMENT of a rural Nebraska county might have just a handful of workers, while Walmart boasts the largest private workforce in the world at over two million employees strong. But both have staffing.

A roofing company might get most of its work by sending salespeople door to door after a hailstorm, while a tech firm in Palo Alto might experiment with the most sophisticated online advertising. But both are engaged in marketing.

A literary agent may work out of her cracker-box apartment in Brooklyn, while a disaster relief nonprofit needs large warehouses on both coasts for trans-shipment of emergency supplies. Yet both have overhead.

Every organization has to think about costs and expenses and record keeping. Every organization conducts strategic thinking and planning of some kind. Every organization has customers, clients, or donors that it needs to serve. These are some of the business basics, and they're virtually universal. They are common elements to any and all business enterprise.

What if there are also some universal best practices common to any and all organizations when it comes to leaving gospel footprints? I know this is tricky and ripe for debate, but I believe there are.

Just as there is a baseline for individuals taking the gospel to work (Chapter 5), so there is a baseline for organizations in treating people and creation in ways that honor God's values.

INDIVIDUAL BLUE SKY	ORGANIZATIONAL BLUE SKY
INDIVIDUAL BASELINE	**ORGANIZATIONAL BASELINE** Chapter 7

In other words, there are some irreducible minimums that apply to any and every organization who want to be and do good. If you want to be part of an organization that lives out the gospel, you must live up to the baseline. And, if you're a Christian, you should want to be part of an organization that, at a minimum, tolerates gospel goodness ... regardless of who's in charge, what you do, and the people you work with. These are the fundamentals that you just don't exception out of if your place of business is going to be a gospel mover.

At this point you might already be objecting:

+ "Ours is a small, privately-owned company, and unless you are a family member, you don't really have an effect on things."
+ "We are a giant public company and we can't do that kind of thing here."
+ "Values are not important in my company."
+ "We just manufacture and don't touch the customer or people much."
+ "We are in an industry that is so upside down and dark—the gospel can't really matter here."
+ "We are a boot-strapping start-up. Once we get bigger we can engage those kinds of things. We are in survival mode right now."

All of these objections may reflect some degree of legitimate concern, and yet I still say that every single organization is capable of operating in some basic ways that allow the gospel to flow. It is possible for all organizations to make baseline gospel impressions regardless of their sector, location, and size, and of whether they're for profit or not for profit, public or private.

"IT IS POSSIBLE FOR
ALL ORGANIZATIONS TO
MAKE BASELINE GOSPEL
IMPRESSIONS REGARDLESS
OF THEIR SECTOR,
LOCATION, AND SIZE, AND
WHETHER THEY'RE FOR
PROFIT OR NOT FOR PROFIT,
PUBLIC OR PRIVATE."

The same gospel minimums apply. I've seen it proved again and again. Whether you are a global Fortune 500 mega company or a single owner-operator dentist or plumber, the organizational baseline applies to you. There is not a company or organization on the planet that could not better itself by tapping into this baseline.

Any organization allowing or attempting a gospel flow-through is anchored to certain common baseline practices. I have identified five foundation stones that, when stacked together, establish the baseline for organizations. I believe any company would improve their standing to build on these five foundations. Here they are. See where your company stands against these:

FOUNDATION STONE 1: A MULTIPLE BOTTOM LINE GUIDES THE COMPANY.

More and more these days, companies are seeing themselves as having more than just a single bottom line—profit. They are trying to achieve other things besides making money. For example, in the triple-bottom-line model, the goals are these:

+ making money
+ treating the environment gently
+ returning good to society

People of faith who are in charge of their business sometimes add a fourth bottom line:

+ revealing God and His ways to people.[2]

But even if an organization does not have an explicitly

spiritual purpose (and never will), it can still reflect acts I and IV of the gospel narrative (Creation and Renewal).

Think about it.

If your company is eager to earn an honorable profit, doesn't that involve obeying the cultural mandate by creating goods or services of worth for your customers?[3]

If you try to reduce waste and follow sustainable business practices, isn't that a way of honoring God's original call to take care of creation?[4]

If your organization tries to take great care of its employees and customers, as well as serve the broader community through some kind of social outreach, isn't it recognizing that people created in the image of God are of inherent value?[5]

So, a part of the baseline of the gospel for organizations is having a multiple bottom line (MBL). If organizations are only about profit, they haven't yet risen to the baseline. Of course profit is crucial. In fact, profit can unlock the other bottom lines, because after all, it's hard to care for people and the planet if you're not financially solvent. But companies begin to reflect gospel basics when they think beyond self-interest to what they can do for the people around them and the world as a whole.[6]

A MBL model of business should be a company's very reason for being. Everyone in the organization should know that they're engaged in more than just making money; they're also doing good for people and for the environment. This understanding will motivate them in their work and guide their decisions.

This framework can become a huge asset and part of the company's value proposition and brand distinction. Think Tom's of Maine (old Toms) and TOMS Shoes (new Toms). Think Whole Foods. Think Patagonia. Some pretty successful companies, right?[7] Simon Sinek helps us grasp the inherent add-on value of these companies, "Any person or organization can explain *what* they do; some can explain *how* they are different or better; but very few can clearly articulate *why*. *Why* is the thing that inspires us and inspires those around us."[8]

Companies that have the welfare of others as a part of their purpose for being have what could be called a "redemptive edge." When they retrofit their facilities to meet green standards, pay their less-skilled employees a living wage, separate from suppliers that use child labor, or do any number of other socially responsible actions, they are having a redemptive affect in the world.

Entrepreneurial brothers Will and Chris Haughey figured out a way to insert magnets into blocks made from Honduran hardwoods. The results are toys that are simple, unique, beautiful, safe, and fun. And through their company, Tegu, the brothers train and employ dozens of workers in Honduras. They also source their wood sustainably and participate in tree replanting programs. With some of their profits, they help to fund a school for children from poor families in the area where Tegu operates its factory.

Will said, "I want Tegu to be phenomenally successful from a commercial and marketplace standpoint. And if the Lord wills, I hope it's used as a great tool and example for others, in terms of inspiring them that they, too, can do something similar, but also in terms of inspiring this country and other developing countries that business can be redeemed. Business can be used in ways that are a blessing to society and ultimately, for Christians, a glory to God."[9]

FOUNDATION STONE 2: A CULTURE OF GRACE AND TRUTH INFUSES THE ORGANIZATION.

Grace and truth are two qualities that do not come naturally to any organization. Don't let the religious silhouette of these terms scare you away from embracing them in your company, regardless of your structure. They are universally useful and can only be built and maintained with serious deliberation and discipline. And yet, when organizations put forth the effort, habits of grace and truth can contribute to forming a happy, productive staff and creating a long-term reputation for trustworthiness in the marketplace.

GRACE

Is grace really something that can live in a fierce business-like culture or it is only part of the DNA of soft-side not-for-profits? What happens in an organization when someone fails to live up to expectations? What about the receptionist who comes in late for work because she's got a problem with her kids? Or what about the new hire who is earnest and works hard but is still taking a long time to learn the ropes? What happens when your usual high performer just doesn't over-deliver this time?

In cases like this, a company with a cutthroat attitude and low tolerance for failure will likely threaten poor work reviews, disciplinary action, or firing.

A company with a culture of grace, on the other hand, will more likely try to understand what's going on in a person's life. It will recognize that it's okay to fail sometimes. It will try to help people through rough patches so that they can return to a higher level of productivity and contribution to the company.

Performance is crucial—but not performance at any and all costs. So although grace does not mean there is no accountability and no consequences for people who are failing, it does mean that we have empathy, fairness, and patience. Grace, expressed like this, can be redemptive, and it almost always builds loyalty over the long term. A graceless culture will eventually turn on itself—and you might be the first in line.

TRUTH

How can an organization traffic in truth?

Let me give you some examples. When an organization has a culture of truth…

…it represents itself accurately to prospective employees, current employees, and customers.

…it is correct and proper when filing tax returns or reporting to investors.

…it admits mistakes and tries to correct them.

…it brings honest accounting of incorrect attitudes and behavior.

…it stands behind its promises even when the bank account isn't flush with cash.

Do you want to know an early signal of an organization that does *not* have a culture of truth? I'll tell you—people in the organization have a habit of parsing the term *honesty*. They ask, "What do you mean by the truth?" and they are quick to find exceptions and loopholes to plain, simple truth telling.

Of course there may be times when we need to withhold information until a more appropriate time. But honest sharing of the truth should always be the default position. We don't need to spend time dissecting the meaning of truth or figuring out ways to get around it. We just need to do it.

I have a client who is running a $100 million construction company. Working in an industry more often known for cutting corners and cutthroat tactics than honesty and full disclosure, this company's leadership is working to build and grow an organization marked by integrity. This isn't a veneer of idealism; it's infused in everything they do. It affects how they talk, how they train, and even how they market themselves. Their core values reinforce and demand it—"We always tell the truth, even when it's a small thing, a hard thing, or it costs us in the end." And most importantly, they live it out. If they make a mistake installing a plumbing, electrical, or HVAC system, they don't pass the buck; they own it. If they notice a problem that an inspector missed, they raise their hand and don't sweep it under the rug.

Is it easy? No. Is it fun? No. There are times when it's painful and costly. There are times when nobody would know if they were a little less than honest. But they've made a decision that truth is an indispensable, non-negotiable part of who they want to be.

And guess what? Turns out it's ultimately good for business. I once asked my friend, the head of this company, about his strategy for acquiring new customers. He pulled out a list of all his current clients and said, "We make sure we do an incredible job with these people in real time." His point was that doing work the right way all the time builds a loyalty that can be traded forward. Truth becomes a strategic advantage.

If grace and truth are going to saturate the culture of an organization, a passion for these qualities has to come from the leaders at the top. In time, people who are the beneficiaries of acts of grace and truth will be more likely to live out grace and truth themselves.

FOUNDATION STONE 3: STEWARDSHIP IS THE PRIMARY MOTIVATOR FOR ALL THINGS PERFORMANCE.

What drives employees to work all weekend to deliver the shipment promised? Why would one company give a portion of its profits away, knowing that this might make it

---

**"TRUTH BECOMES A
STRATEGIC ADVANTAGE."**

---

less competitive? What motivates one employee to stay late to finish a report while the rest of the team runs off to happy hour? How do the leaders of any company arrange their assets for peak performance?

Every organization must determine how to get their best ROI (return on investment) from all the assets working on behalf of the company. To do that with any consistency, they must harness the powerful concept of motivation, or "why I do what I do." One super motivator seems to float above all motivators when applied to life and work. It is the glue holding all other motivations in check. It is stewardship.

I love the definition that Peter Block introduced in his groundbreaking book back in 1993 on stewardship—"It is to hold something in trust for another." He went on to say, "Historically, stewardship was a means to protect a kingdom while those rightfully in charge were away, or, more often to govern for the sake of an underage king. The underage king is the next generation." Now that sounds pretty familiar. Looking around the corner and down the track ahead of my current scope (the next generation) is core to the idea of popular themes of stewardship and sustainability. Block finishes by saying, "Stewardship is the willingness to be accountable by operating out of service rather than control."[10]

It means looking at all your assets as if you are holding them in trust for another and you are responsible for investing them wisely for a long-term return. Stewardship locks me to the long view and it shifts the focus from being all about me to include your agenda as well. Stewardship makes tomorrow as important as today.

When people of faith are leading organizations, they may consider themselves to be stewarding the resources of their organization for God, the King, who has left for a season.

But even when the leadership of an organization has no faith orientation, they can think of themselves as being stewards on behalf of humanity's common good or the next generation. Either way, it's a bigger, more generous way to approach resource management.

Stewardship doesn't mean being cautious to the point of fearfully hoarding assets. On the contrary, it is about leveraging your assets, risking them for a greater gain.[11]

Managing, leveraging, and stewarding people might be the most complicated of all asset management. I have heard and agree there are only three possible tools to extract optimum performance out of your team.[12]

Coercion—Forcing someone to do what you want by use of intimidation or threats. Sadly, entire industries have been built around coercion. And unfortunately, it can work too, at least for a while … until it starts to backfire.

Incentive—This is the if/then approach. "If you increase your sales, then your commission will go up." "If you streamline your departmental budget, then you'll see a bonus in your paycheck." This is a better option than coercion, and sometimes it works, but it can be costly and complicated to implement.

Inspiration—This involves showing people how they are part of something bigger and exciting, then enlisting their active support in it. It is based on finding the best in others and matching it to the best for others. It doesn't necessarily have to replace incentives, but it has the power to motivate people even when the motivation money has dried up. Inspiration is the most universal and powerful tool that any leader in any organization has. And the best companies with consistent superior culture and performance tap into it.

I hope you'll agree with me that inspiration is the highest level in the art and discipline of people management. But how do we do it? How do we motivate people?

We know the best of all motivators is intrinsic. And the purest of all intrinsic motivations brings us back to stewardship. Stewardship is me caring for you and your future with the level of energy I care for myself and my future. Stewardship makes me figure out what your dreams and aspirations are and help you realize them. Stewardship is the posture that holds things. But not too tightly. It is responsible but not possessive.

Stewardship may be an overused term, but I am convinced it is an under-utilized driver of behavior when applied to organizational culture and performance.

FOUNDATION STONE 4: HUMBLE COLLABORATION IS A PART OF EVERYDAY BEHAVIOR.

Some institutional leaders are little more than business bullies. Some organizations are battlefields for turf wars fought both inside and outside the walls of the company.

Internally, the spirit of competition can be a good thing. But it can also be a devil of division. In some companies, promotion comes through a kind of social Darwinism where predator vanquishes prey—*I win, you lose.*

In contrast, companies that reflect a gospel baseline recognize the value of working together and not thinking too highly of oneself. In *Collaborate!: The Art of We*, Dan Sanker defines collaboration as, "the synergistic relationship formed when two or more entities working together produce something much greater than the sum of their individual abilities and contributions."[13] Collaboration is people getting stuff done together rather than in isolated silos. The motivation, process, and outcome differ dramatically.

Organizations should be like orchestras full of musicians playing together to produce a marvelous symphony. Organizations should have an expectation that people will get a check in the "plays well with others" box and won't waste time reinventing a wheel that someone else already knows how to make.

Ed Catmull, CEO of moviemaker Pixar, wrote about the collaborative process in his company. "People at all levels support one another. Everyone is fully invested in helping everyone else turn out the best work. They really do feel that it's all for one and one for all."[14]

In an extreme example, at ING Direct Canada, the employees have few titles and very few strict organizational lines. Anyone can talk to anyone else, and leaders focus on removing obstacles instead of creating them.[15]

There are lots of ways for organizations to create collaborative environments that honor each employee's worth and bring out the best contribution each one can make. They don't have to lose the directive power of leadership or put the company's business strategy at risk. But people must be humble and open to learn from and work synergistically with others to collaborate. Some might even term this *servant leadership*.

The idea of collaboration actually is even more powerful when applied outside the company walls. Collaboration can be a freeway system for the gospel to travel. Non-collaboration can be a disappointing dead end or stifling roadblock. The gospel flows best when a company understands its role and

"COLLABORATION CAN BE A FREEWAY SYSTEM FOR THE GOSPEL TO TRAVEL. NON-COLLABORATION CAN BE A DISAPPOINTING DEAD END OR STIFLING ROADBLOCK."

then embraces the fact that it is only a *part* of the whole, not the whole. It is common for organizations to not collaborate with others who are already doing similar work and they want to do it all. And ironically, some of the biggest violators can be our not-for-profit friends. Often our unbridled ambition and appetite push us up and down the supply chain, aspiring to be all parts of a solution. Sure, it might garner us a bit more profit or recognition, but is that the smartest, most sustainable approach? Instead, we should be looking for someone to partner and collaborate with.

I firmly believe we have lost the symphonic tone of collaboration today in most workspaces. The pursuit of competitive advantage has replaced working with others to accomplish a greater good. Eventually an unhealthy independence can eat through a company's culture. But just as truly, rebuilding a collaborative strategy can make a company succeed while contributing to God's process of social renewal. And it can deliver surprising outcomes. One professor of psychology said it this way: "All great inventions emerge from a long sequence of small sparks; the first idea isn't all that good, but thanks to collaboration it later sparks another idea, or it's reinterpreted in an unexpected way. Collaboration brings sparks together to generate breakthrough innovations."[16] We have long believed that collective wisdom is extremely powerful. Collaboration is simply structuring to create that.

Think about it: In your organization, are you more competitive or collaborative? What is the last example you saw of collaboration benefiting the common good?

FOUNDATION STONE 5: WORKERS ARE TREATED AS HUMAN BEINGS, NOT AS TOOLS FOR TRANSACTIONS.

Organizations develop a reputation for how they treat people. Both those within an organization and those looking at it from the outside form an opinion about how the organization views and uses its employees. What's your organization's reputation when it comes to its human resources?

In the worst cases, organizations treat employees not like human beings at all but rather like material assets that are useful insofar as they help the organization meet its financial goals. If employees are deemed to be no longer useful, they are cast aside without concern. It's all about results at any costs. It's about the competitive edge, about winning. It's about the organization's goals, not someone's personal situation.

If the head of a sales team has an attitude that says, "All I need are thirty-five warm bodies in here racking up a sales growth of fifteen percent," there's a problem. The members of that sales team are *people* after all.

What about a law firm that dangles partnership in front of its new associates and forces them to turn practically every hour of the day into billable time, until they wake up one day and they're in their thirties and they realize they have no life?

I recently had a 1Day Strategy Lab with an executive who had burned out in a high-demand/high-reward investment banking and venture capital company.[17] During his run, he was building a new house (worth multiple millions) and was told by the older partners in the firm, "The bigger, the better." They were inadvertently saying, "It will just enslave you to our system that much more."

An organization that values people will demonstrate care

by how it motivates people (coercion, incentives, inspiration), how it pays people, how it communicates with people, how it tells the truth. It will treat them with kindness, fairness, dignity, justice, and compassion. Some like to pull out the Golden Rule—it comes down to treating others as you would want to be treated yourself.

Some companies set aside an emergency fund to help employees who are going through a tragedy. Other companies pay for their employees' children to go to college. Still others collect money at Christmas to help workers who don't have enough money to buy Christmas presents. There is no single way to treat people humanely. It depends. But if there is not a tension over this issue at the executive level, the company might score low in this area.

The point is that organizations are intentional about treating people decently. We genuinely care for and hurt for those less fortunate in such a way that it causes us to pause and leads us to make a sacrifice in some manner. But we don't just cry when others cry and laugh when others laugh; we structure into our company platforms and mechanisms for our people and friends to engage others in need.

I have long enjoyed the writings of Irish author/philosopher Charles Handy. He repeatedly ranks second only to Peter Drucker as the leading thinker of organizational behavior and management of the last century. In *The Hungry Spirit* he prophetically proclaimed, "Business, and indeed all institutions, are communities not properties, and their inhabitants are to be more properly thought of as citizens rather than employees or human resources."[18] Certainly this idea must be held in tension with its balancing reality on the opposite side, but there is a genius kernel of the gospel that is embedded in his approach to people.

One reliable indicator of whether an organization is treating workers as human beings is how they let people go. If someone is no longer needed in the company, will the company show them the door as soon as possible? Or will they try to be compassionate, such as by expressing gratitude for what the worker has done for the organization, providing generous severance, and offering assistance in finding another job? I know this is not a simple issue, and in a litigious society things must be done with caution. But a redemptive edge can be applied to the communication and process of letting someone go. I just watched a company "downsize" half its employees in order to survive and reboot for another season of existence in a gospel-minded manner. It can be done.

Another thing that gospel-minded organizations do is see people, not only as individual contributors to the company's goals, but as people who want to develop and are connected with others outside of work. Most workers have family members who need some of their time and attention. Will your company respect that?

Henry Kaestner and I serve on a board together and have become friends. He is one of the cofounders of Bandwidth. com, a company that helps businesses find Internet connectivity. Recently I heard him talk about how his company tries to help its employees balance their work and family/friendship responsibilities:

> We've got three hundred employees, most of whom are young families. We firmly believe that you've got an opportunity to be a parent from six to eight [o'clock] and those are really, really important [times]. So there's no glory in staying late at Bandwidth.com. In fact, we go around and we kick people out of the office. ...

At the same time we want to compete and win. We want to do
excellent, excellent business. So when there's work to be done, it
means dialing back in at eight o'clock and continuing to hammer.[18]

START HERE

I know you are eager to dream and stretch toward the blue
sky of your organization living out the gospel, and we'll be
getting to that in the next chapter. But postpone that endeavor
until you help the organization get anchored to the baselines.
A building won't last unless it's established on a strong base.

So let's quickly review. The five foundation stones
establishing an organizational baseline are

- a multiple bottom line that guides the company
- a culture of grace and truth that marks the organization
- stewardship as the primary motivator for all things
  performance
- humble collaboration as a part of everyday behavior
- treatment of workers as human beings rather than tools
  for transactions

Does your organization have room for improvement in any
of these areas?

I'd be surprised if it didn't.

Now think about your own zone of influence within your
organization. How can you to start nudging your organization
in a more gospel-minded direction? You may be "only" a low-
level manager, but you can encourage collaboration within
your team. You may be an executive with layers of influence,
and so maybe you need to revisit the powerful fuel of
stewardship. You may be a business owner and need to shore
up your multiple bottom line.

Do what you can, wherever you find yourself in the organization, to build its baseline. If others on the team are like-minded, you might find that eventually your organization is resting on a solid basis for not only producing great goods or services but also treating nature and humanity respectfully.

From there, the baselines can propel you into the blue sky.

"A GRACELESS CULTURE
WILL EVENTUALLY TURN ON
ITSELF AND YOU MIGHT BE
THE FIRST IN LINE."

CHAPTER 8

EXTRAORDINARY ORGANIZATIONS

> *"There are no rules of architecture for a castle in the clouds."*[1]
> —G. K. Chesterton

FORTUNE MAGAZINE HAS its Fortune 500 list of the five hundred largest companies in America, ranked by revenue. Sometimes I wonder if somebody should come up with a listing of the top five hundred gospel-minded organizations. I know it would be a slippery assignment sorting out measurements and opinions about each company, because gospel effectiveness isn't as quantifiable as revenue. But I suspect we all know for-profit and not-for-profit organizations that are doing an extraordinary job as agents of renewal and that would easily make the list.

In this chapter you'll learn about a few of the organizations that would get my vote for inclusion in the Gospel 500 if such a list existed. These organizations illustrate, not just a compliance with the baseline discussed in the last chapter, but also a customized effort of gospel expression in their particular vertical. They have raised their hand to ask questions alongside the tax collectors and the soldiers in the narrative with John the Baptist. In other words, they have found their "gospel hot spots" and linked up to a level of purpose, as well as renewal in their community and the world, that is impressive.

A DIVERSITY OF GOSPEL EXPRESSIONS

The U.S. Bureau of Labor Statistics uses a standard occupational classification that segregates workers into 840 detailed occupations. These are further classified into 461 broad occupations, 97 minor groups, and 23 major groups.[2]

Michael Robinson, founder and chief career coach at

CareerPlanner.com, compiled a list of more than twelve thousand job titles and job descriptions. They include able seaman, academic dean, accordion tuner, accounting clerk, acrobat, and advertising clerk—all without even pushing very far into the list of jobs that start with A.[3]

And even as there are a lot of different kinds of workers, so there are a lot of different kinds of workplaces. Think about the variables here—size, verticals, structure, culture, values, geography, services, and products.

+ Working in New York City is not the same as working in Fayetteville, Arkansas.
+ Working the night shift is not the same as working in the day.
+ Working in a small, agile start-up is not the same as working for a large, mature company.
+ Working in a public company is not the same as working in a private company.
+ Being the CEO or other senior leader is not the same as having a job way down in the org chart.
+ Work is not the same when you are using your own money to fuel company growth as it is when you are using someone else's money.
+ Working in an organization that is in growth mode is not the same as working in one that is in pause mode.
+ Working in a company that sells chicken is not the same as working in one that sells Bibles.
+ Work is not the same when you have a life-giving team culture as it is when you have an oppressive, dark culture.

Why am I saying all this? Here's the reason: because our jobs and our organizations are so diverse, their expressions of the gospel are going to be diverse as well. A one-size-fits-all answer will not work when you are looking to leverage the gospel message to a particular work setting. You've got to figure out what the gospel might look like when it expresses itself through your particular organization at any particular time.

WHAT PART OF THE BLUE SKY ARE YOU IN?

I'm going to begin helping you answer the question of how to make your organization a Gospel 500 organization. As I do so, keep in mind a few assumptions I am making.

First, I'm assuming that you have a genuine interest in flowing the gospel through your organization. My intention all along in this book has been to address people and organizations that are mindful of the reach, power, and intent of the gospel going to work. I am not trying to explore those unconscious faith instruments of goodness and renewal that God uses in spite of their stubborn resistance.

Second, the ways in which a particular organization can express the gospel are endless. Why? Because the mixture of kinds of work, different organizations, and contexts are limitless in today's work world.

Third, there is no order of significance or rank in the gospel blue sky, only a variety of expression. Even though it would be fun to corral five hundred gospel-minded companies, I really don't think you can rank gospel effectiveness from one to five hundred. But always keep it clear: the single biggest distinction in both the baseline and the blue sky is the supernatural muscle of God's Spirit. It is God doing God's work, not human beings trying to do God's work in our own strength and intelligence. So there will always be a mysterious, non-formulaic element to gospel growth.

With that said, I believe gospel-minded companies fall

into one of three macro regions in the blue sky. In other words, there are three qualifiers separating company A from companies B and C. Figure out where your organization fits on the gospel blue-sky map by asking yourself the following three questions:

REGION 1. IS THE GOSPEL MESSAGE UNDER THE RADAR?

If you answer *yes* to that question, then your business or nonprofit does not produce goods or services that are visibly connected with the gospel. Nor does faith-talk enter into how the organization is run in a public manner. Yet one or more people of influence in the organization may aspire to help the organization operate in a way that is distinctly honoring to God. They want their company to be a gospel conduit, even though it must be done away from the spotlight. Most public company leaders with any gospel intentionality operate within Region 1 of the blue sky. They have to because of their structure.

The French-born reformer John Calvin talked much about the gospel going to work in the details of daily life. He urged all workers to plant a gospel seed in broad ways when he said, "All men were created to busy themselves with labor … for the common good."[4] But it is often subtle. The gospel is not always loud and overt. It doesn't always have to hang on the corridor walls, sing in the lobby music, or scream from the website. It's more embedded than that. What company is in Region 1? Think any secular-facing organization with a gospel-minded leader in an influence seat.

You may wonder if there really are leaders and influencers within the great corporations of the world, such as Coca-Cola, Google, and Facebook, who go to work every day with the intention of living out their faith in their work. I can assure you there are many such people. I know a lot of them, including people in the three corporations I just named. Although I need to respect their privacy by not identifying them here, there are many people of active faith in the major secular organizations of this world. They prove that Region 1 is a viable part of the gospel blue sky.

REGION 2. IS FAITH A PUBLIC INFORMER AND GUIDE FOR THE LANGUAGE, CULTURE, AND OPERATIONS OF YOUR ORGANIZATION?

If you answered *yes* to this question, then although your organization may not offer overtly faith-oriented goods or services, the gospel definitely helps to shape the culture, values, and decisions of the organization. Anyone on the inside will inevitably hear about God or the Bible or biblical values and it is common for faith-speak to flow through the personality and style of its leadership. The organization has been imprinted by the gospel, and this is evident to those who touch the company on any front.

This situation is common for private companies owned by a faith follower or by a sole proprietor who is shaped by his or her faith. Think dentist, doctor, lawyer, plumber, or landscape architect who happens to be visible and outspoken regarding faith. Think any size private company with one or more vocal and intentional faith followers in top leadership. They are structurally free to shout the gospel at any volume they desire, as long as they can live with the outcomes.

Two clear examples of a Region 2 company are Chick-fil-A and Hobby Lobby. Companies like these do great work with the gospel program running in the background of their operating system. And they usually don't mind allowing the gospel sound to show up in a public way periodically.

REGION 3. DOES YOUR ORGANIZATION HAVE A SERVICE OR PRODUCT OFFERING THAT IS OVERTLY FAITH ORIENTED OR DRIVEN?

If so, then the gospel presumably permeates the inner workings of your organization as well as the image it presents to the outside. You could be working as a Christian counselor, selling Bibles, leading a church, or running a faith-based not-for-profit. Your public "reason for being" is to promote faith. You might even categorize your organization as a "ministry" or "Christian business." You likely see spiritual impact as core to your organization's reason for being. (Notice I said your organization's reason for being, not your personal reason for being.) Evangelism and discipleship are your primary drivers, regardless of what you might label them. Your organization is thoroughly colored by the gospel and exists to expand the canvas of the gospel. When you think of Region 3, think organizations like Catalyst, LifeWay, Passion Conferences, and Praxis. (I am highlighting some of the larger organizations, knowing full well there are countless other organizations that could be highlighted.)

My point is not that one region of the blue sky is better than another in terms of propagating the gospel. Any region can be a gospel carrier. But it will vary in expression and guidelines. The list of things you can do, can't do, and must do becomes the single greatest differentiator in the organizational blue sky. This is where you find your boundaries and guard rails in the discussion.

Some leaders in some companies can pray publicly with people during a crisis. Others can't.

Some organizations can direct a percentage of their profits toward faith-based causes at the end of each year. Others can't.

Some organizations can visibly reflect the owners' and leaders' personal faith journey. Others can't.

Some companies can actively link their growth and expansion to kingdom opportunities. (For example, I recently observed a company that stretched its operational reach to India because of the vision and faith of its leaders.) Other companies can't do that.

The blue sky accommodates the differences among organizations. Although every company can and should be practicing the baselines, the more customized expressions of the gospel in the blue sky run the gamut.

Keep in mind, too, that most of the Gospel 500 (or Gospel 1,000 or even Gospel 10,000) are organizations that you and I have never heard of. They are only known in their particular community. It is a local coffee and donut shop, a family-owned construction company, a dentist or a realtor carrying the gospel to work in the blue sky of their niche. They are applying the gospel day in and day out to the details of work without a lot of publicity and fanfare. But the customers in that community know it, see it, and feel the gospel in some fashion.

One way or another, that's what we want to accomplish, regardless of which of the three regions we're working in.

NAVIGATING THE BLUE SKY

Knowing what region of the blue sky your organization occupies is one thing. Figuring out how to specifically promote the gospel within that region and in your particular industry is another.

The best way to get started, as in the individual blue sky, is to look at the "gospel gaps" in your organization. Ask yourself: *What is my organization doing that is not compatible with gospel values, and how could we change that? Where are the lines defining the true, the good, or the beautiful in our space being blurred? Where are the seven deadly sins running rampant and ripe for a gospel touch of salt and light, perfume and leaven?*

The founder of Elevation Burger, a fast-food franchise, is a Christian who wants to put the gospel to work in his burger chain. Yet they are operating in an industry that plays on people's gluttonous desire for food that tastes good but is bad for your health. Elevation's response was to make their burgers out of organic, grass-fed, free-range beef and to cook their fries in olive oil. So much healthier. And the food still tastes great! He found a gap and filled it.

Do you think God is honored by a fast-food company that is trying to offer healthier food and treat people and the environment better? I do. I know this might stretch a two-story gospel mindset, but give it a try.

Companies of all types, in all sorts of places, are turning things around in a gospel direction. I want to tell you about two companies—one in the automotive industry and one in the financial industry—that are finding the gospel gaps and bridging their work to their faith.

THE GOSPEL ON THE CAR LOT

Car sales organizations are some of the most vilified companies in our economy. Fairly or not, they're widely suspected of using shady techniques and a superior knowledge of automobile costs to get an advantage over customers who are just trying to negotiate a reasonable deal on a new ride. I confess there have been times when I have wondered if there could be a single person of genuine mature faith working on a car lot anywhere in the country.

"ASK YOURSELF: WHAT IS MY ORGANIZATION DOING THAT IS NOT COMPATIBLE WITH GOSPEL VALUES, AND HOW COULD WE CHANGE THAT? WHERE IS THE TRUE, THE GOOD, OR THE BEAUTIFUL BEING BLURRED? WHERE ARE THE SEVEN DEADLY SINS RUNNING RAMPANT AND RIPE FOR A GOSPEL TOUCH OF SALT AND LIGHT?"

But that was before I met Don Flow. Don is a car salesman who has done as incredible a job of applying the gospel through his company as anyone I know.

If it's possible to live out the gospel in Don's line of work, it's possible to do the same in *any* work arena!

Back in 1957, Don's father opened a car dealership in Winston-Salem, North Carolina. Today Don is CEO of Flow Companies, which has grown to thirty-seven dealerships in North Carolina and Virginia, employing over a thousand workers and selling automobiles from twenty carmakers. It is one of the most successful car dealership groups in the nation.

Don has thought deeply about how he can make the gospel infuse the work he and his employees do. One approach he has chosen is to eliminate the possibility of negotiation shenanigans entirely. Every new or used car dealership in the Flow group offers full transparency about the products it is offering and puts a single price on each car. There is never any price negotiation or "I have to go talk to my manager about the deal." The number is ... the number.

What Don is doing, in my opinion, is converting a gospel gap to a gospel hot spot. What is the gospel gap? Namely, the dealer has all the information and data and the customer is always operating in the position of weakness. That power posture is the currency of the car salesman. Don pushed the gospel into that dark spot of the canvas and is painting truth and dignity.

In a presentation at Seattle Pacific University a few years ago, Don posed the question, "How are you supposed to live love in the workplace?"[5] Here is a part of his answer:

It means that we put relationships ahead of transactions and that we relate to every customer like a valued friend. When we do this, we re-personalize the marketplace. Customers are not profit-maximizing opportunities; they are real people with real problems that we are serving.

The first commitment is that the customer is always assumed to be deserving of extraordinary personal service even if they don't always prove to be so. For us to make this real, we must be a place that keeps our promises and always does what's right for the customer. We must treat every single person who walks into the showroom, the service lane, the parts department, the body shop like a valued friend, like a guest in our home, regardless of their station in life.

The Flow Companies are not perfect, of course, any more than are any of the other companies I name in this book. But they're genuinely attempting to apply love to their work in a way that reflects a four-act gospel and fills in the open spaces of God's big canvas. And they do it in a way that is tailored to their own particular kind of business.

THE GOSPEL IN THE FINANCIAL INDUSTRY

Michael Bontrager has always been gifted in financial matters. He's got a B-school degree and did a stint on Wall Street. But when his childhood faith was reactivated in adulthood, he decided that he wanted to change the way people think about finance and about those who work in finance. He was asking the John the Baptist question applied to the world of finance.

In 1991 Mike founded Chatham Financial, a global financial firm specializing in the complicated business of debt and derivative investments. He works in an industry that very often is all about unbridled selfishness and the accumulation of wealth without regard for what it does to people and the world. *What would it look like*, Mike wonders, *for a financial company to make a remarkable profit while doing good along the way for employees, customers, and the world at large?*

Chatham is a multiple-bottom-line company that strives to not only make money but also to operate with fairness, humility, and service. It provides many forms of charitable giving and community outreach, and it tries to help employees thrive over the long term.

Consider what this means to hiring.

Mike wants to hire some of the very best financial minds to work for Chatham. But how can he compete with Wall Street firms, which offer seven-figure salaries and seven-figure bonuses to their best employees? Well, Mike decided that he could do Wall Street one better by offering top candidates what he calls an *absolute good* in place of the *relative good* of the financial rewards and perks that the traditional financial firms can offer.

Money—even with a lot of zeroes involved—is a relative good when it stands alone as a scorecard. The chasing of money alone will always leave someone on the shorter side of the comparison. We tend to compare up, not down. We don't measure our bounty against someone well below our level and find genuine happiness and thankfulness. Rather, at bonus time, we measure up to those who made much more, wishing we had their fortune. Relative goodness is slippery. It always has been, always will be.

Chatham offers an absolute good to employees, says Mike, because when you work there, you are not only earning a very good income (though perhaps not as much as on Wall Street), but also you are helping others and are able to have a healthy, well-rounded life. This package is more valuable than the biggest Christmas bonus handed out in profit-obsessed financial firms on Wall Street.

But don't mistake Mike's ambition to build a great world-class company. And don't think he has assembled some narrow-minded company culture. He has people of all faiths and backgrounds tied into his particular gospel hot spot within the financial industry. One of their cultural guidelines is to be a "faith friendly but belief neutral environment." I think this is a genius way to keep the doors and windows open for ongoing vigorous gospel dialogue.

My friend Mike is all about finding effective ways to do good in a sector that's always been more interested in making more.

THE CULMINATION

Ask any person of faith who is a part of an organization like Elevation Burger, the Flow Companies, or Chatham Financial—that is, any organization that's embedding gospel values in a creative and customized way—and you'll soon learn that it's thrilling to be a part of!

However, it is crucial that we don't create too narrow a litmus test for leaders and organizations attempting to find any gospel footing of the true, the good, and the beautiful. It will not, and frankly should not, look the same across the board. I was reminded of this when having lunch with Doug McMillan, the current CEO of Walmart Stores. Doug started at Walmart when he was seventeen, and he's been trying to serve the company and its customers ever since. But he is also a man who has tried to serve his deep personal faith in Jesus as a worker in a huge global public company. How does that look? What he can do, can't do, and must do might vary from another CEO down the street. We have to give leaders and organizations room to explore and personalize their practice in the blue sky. That is crucial. Sure there are some individual and even organizational commonalities for every worker, whether you are Doug at the top or Steve at the bottom. But there is also a huge blue sky open for personal exploration. Making this a one-size-fits-all dulls our spiritual imagination and ultimately short bottles up the salt, light, perfume, and leaven and keeps them from being the catalytic force they were intended.

Could *your* organization do a better job of putting down the footprints of the gospel in the world? I invite you to dream about how your business or nonprofit can do amazing things that channel the gospel into the narrative. That's the gospel blue sky for organizations.

Jack Dorsey, co-founder of Twitter, has said, "The most efficient means to spread an idea today is a corporate structure; 200 years ago it was probably something different; 100 years from now it will be something completely different."[6]

Organizations are powerful. We can't neglect them when we think about God's desire to paint His truth across the big canvas of our lives and His world.

We all must ask and answer, "How does the gospel go to work in my industry and especially in my particular organization?" This is the most penetrating question anyone can ask in his or her faith and work. It requires vulnerable personalization. And it demonstrates a mature faith that depends on God doing His work His way.

Ask it.

"THE GOSPEL IS NOT
ALWAYS LOUD AND OVERT.
IT DOESN'T ALWAYS HAVE
TO HANG ON THE CORRIDOR
WALLS, SING IN THE LOBBY
MUSIC, OR SCREAM FROM
THE WEBSITE.
IT'S MORE EMBEDDED
THAN THAT."

CHAPTER 9

BOTH-AND

> *"The problem with Western Christians is not that they aren't where they should be but that they aren't what they should be where they are."*[1]
> —Os Guinness

WE STARTED THIS book with two preachers named John.

In Chapter 1, the church planter John pointed us to the question that so many people of faith should be asking: *Do I understand and embrace the power, reach, and full intent of the gospel as it impacts the details of my everyday life?* And because work covers so much of the canvas of our time and energy, the implied follow-up question is: *How does the gospel go to work?*

In Chapter 4, John the Baptist faced questions from assorted workers and then gave answers with surprising job specificity. He told us to start by embracing the universal baseline of gospel expressions that apply to all workers in all settings. Then he launched into the blue sky, where we contextualize the gospel against personality, job, and work setting.

The same baseline + blue-sky formula works for us as individual people of faith *and* for our organizations. This framework helps us move beyond conventional thinking tied to the bottom left quadrant and pushes us to find the edges of the gospel in our diverse work. It anchors us to the non-negotiables, but also opens the door to dreaming big about gospel impact.

My final piece of advice, then, is to remember that this is not an either/or proposition. You don't merely live up to the baseline, nor solely explore the blue sky. It's both-and.

You'll never graduate from the gospel baseline any more than an athlete can ignore the fundamentals of his game play and expect to keep winning. The baseline is the foundation on which you build. Let it slip, and you will lose your credibility and your platform for anything you want to try in the blue sky.

So never neglect the baseline.

But don't stop there either.

Consider it a major part of your faith development, as well as your God-given mission in this life, to figure out how to particularize the gospel within your own wiring and apply it to your particular company or organization. Be an explorer to push the frontiers of redemption and renewal in your workplace. Perhaps you'll chart new territory where other people can follow.

KEEP ASKING AND ANSWERING THE QUESTION

One day not long ago I was in New York for a conference of Christian leaders and got into a car with my buddy Jason Locy, a branding/design strategist from Manhattan. With us was Dave K., co-owner of the home décor company DEMDACO. You may remember him from Chapter 2.

Dave had just given a terrific talk about faith at work, encouraging the men and women gathered at the conference to practice honesty, treat their employees well, and create cultures that invite gospel values. He was basically arguing for the individual and organizational baselines.

During the car ride, Jason asked Dave a couple of penetrating questions: "Dave, how does the gospel shape your concept of design? How does it affect your view of consumption?" In other words, Jason was pushing Dave to articulate what it means for the gospel to go to work with him as a manufacturer supplying the global retailer market. He was pushing past the baseline to the blue sky to the hard question of particular application.

From there, the conversation moved into some fascinating topics involved in making tasteful, durable home décor products while earning a profit. But the specifics of Dave's answer aren't what matter most to the rest of us. What matters is that we were exploring what it looks like to contextualize the gospel in a deeper, more specific manner. We were exploring forward, not just resting on past sentiments.

You see, in that car were four men who had all already spent considerable time thinking about faith-work interaction, yet we still had a lot to learn from each other when bringing the sharp edge of the gospel to bear on a particular industry. We were pushing each other to grow in this area. We were considering new ideas, challenging our own assumptions, and refusing to settle for easy answers.

Another example came in a late-night email exchange with an executive friend in a large company. I asked him how his gospel edges were doing. He recounted things he was doing to maintain his moral authority, which gave him the right to shake out the salt and flip on the light. Love that baseline dedication. But then he went into his blue sky of gospel application.

In his specific case, he decided the most strategic gospel hot spot was mentoring teams below him in the organization. He facilitates six to eight different groups each month across the company. In each meeting he weaves in his faith and values while grooming the next layer of executives. He tries to answer the *why* behind the *what* and the *how*. In a 24/7 work culture driven by "sink or swim" and a "go fast and break things" mindset, he has found his gospel hot spots. My friend is tethered to the baseline but soaring in the blue sky.

This is what all people of faith should be doing regularly. Our assignment is to anchor down to both baselines. But at the same time we want to ask the question of John the Baptist connecting the gospel to our particular wiring and our specific industry hot spots—not just once, but over and over again.

NO EXEMPTIONS

The gospel is intended to penetrate, permeate, and alter the way we consider our work and do our work. Its reach, power, and intent are staggering, stretching even our greatest spiritual imagination. And because our work covers so much of the canvas of our lives, applying this gospel can be revolutionary—even for veterans of the faith. It is the gospel story that transforms the hearts of people. And one single transformed heart can inject the salt, light, and sweet perfume that can alter an entire company culture over time. Kingdom movement happens when the gospel goes to work.

And when the gospel does this through you and your organization, all kinds of wonderful things are going to start happening. Your work life will give you a sense of fulfillment and purpose like you've never known. You will begin to understand the grace of God in a new way. Your heart for those unfamiliar with faith will be both broken and warmed at the same time. Your faith will grow as you watch God at work.

Concerned about the darkness and dullness of the world? Bring it light and salt. Have a passion for people who are less than they could be and getting nowhere? Bring perfume and leaven.

When we engage as a community correctly, the gospel always flows. And when the complete gospel—the four-act gospel—flows, our families, neighborhoods, churches, companies, communities, and nations are changed.

In the end, work is too important a part of our lives to exempt it from our joy and our responsibility of giving glory to

"THE GOSPEL IS INTENDED
TO PENETRATE, PERMEATE,
AND ALTER THE WAY WE
CONSIDER OUR WORK
AND DO OUR WORK."

God. And so there is never an exception for the gospel going to work.

- It's never too early and it's never too late to take the gospel to work.
- You're never too young and you're never too old to take the gospel to work.
- Your work is never too simple and it's never too complicated to take the gospel to work.
- Your organization is never too small and it's never too big to take the gospel to work.
- Your work setting is never too religious and it's never too secular to take the gospel to work.

As a reformer, philanthropist, and long-term member of the British Parliament, William Wilberforce was the perfect illustration of someone being faithful to the baselines but also pioneering the gospel into territory normally improbable. And before you assume he lived in an easy time of history, think again. Nothing happening in our culture and in our businesses today is more challenging that what Wilberforce faced. During his time in leadership, Britain was the mind and muscle of human trafficking (slave trade) worldwide. It was so entrenched that even people of faith had learned to turn a blind eye to it. But William Wilberforce and his band of associates refused to let the gospel gaps grow any wider.

What anchored him? His understanding and conviction of the reach, power, and intent of the gospel narrative. "As he sat at his desk that foggy Sunday morning in 1787 thinking about his conversion and his calling, Wilberforce asked and answered a pivotal question. Had God saved him only to rescue his own soul from hell? He could not accept that. If Christianity was true and meaningful, it must not only save but serve."[2] Yes, the gospel saved his personal soul. But the gospel wasn't only to be "consumed" by William. It was to serve all of humanity in redemption and renewal. To serve was to find the gospel gaps in his particular industry (politics and government) and convert them to gospel hot spots. William Wilberforce spent his adult life doing just that.

A more recent hero of faith going to work was Bob Briner, author of *Roaring Lambs*. I remember being with him in his home one Saturday morning discussing his passion to fill the gospel gaps in the entertainment and media industries. Bob deeply believed, "if a religion is really vital, meaningful, relevant, and important, it will make a difference not only in the individuals but also in the society itself."[3]

I firmly believe there are gospel and work heroes in every city and community around the world. We just don't know them all. However, those who traffic in their world do. Those who work next to them and live in community with them know them as salt, light, and the sweet perfume of the gospel. You might not have books written about you or even be recognized as a faith work leader. But when any person of faith tethers their life and work to the baselines, and then they begin to courageously explore the blue sky of particular gospel work application, kingdom energy happens. The gospel's power, reach, and intent is revolutionary, even for veterans of the faith.

"WE ARE GOD'S HANDIWORK,
CREATED IN CHRIST JESUS
TO DO GOOD WORKS,
WHICH GOD PREPARED
IN ADVANCE FOR US TO DO."
– EPHESIANS 2:10 NIV

THINK ABOUT IT

1. How would you score yourself on understanding and practicing the reach, power, and intent of the gospel in the details of daily life?

2. Where are your gospel gaps? What part, or parts, of your work would benefit from a "gospel injection"? What would it look like to bring the reach, power, and intent of the gospel to your whole life?

3. What is your purpose in life? And how does the gospel go to work with you?

4. Do you believe and practice a two-act gospel or a four-act gospel? What's the evidence for that?

5. What connection do you see between the Bible's cultural mandate and your own work?

6. How many hours do you spend at work each week, on average? How mindful and intentional are you regarding the power and reach of the gospel in the details of your work?

7. How has your approach to work changed over the years? How might those changes impact the way you consider the gospel going to work with you?

8. What are your mental "bad boxes" when it comes to work and the gospel?

9. Placing yourself in the narrative today, what is your particular industry question for John the Baptist (as it were), and what might he say?

10. What are your initial questions about the gospel baseline and the blue sky at work? About applying the gospel on an individual and an organizational basis at work?

11. What can you learn from non-Christians in the business world about doing good for humanity?

12. Would those you work with validate the claim that your attitude and habits reflect an eternal link and mission?

13. Have you grown in character development, or are you struggling with the same old issues you have been wrestling with for decades?

14. Have you lost the sharp edge of excellence in all you do in your work? Why or why not?

15. Would your co-workers say you have interest and energy in their world, or would they write you off as only self-serving?

16. What generation do you belong to? How has your membership in this generation shaped you? As a part of this generation, how are you best equipped to leverage the gospel where you work?

17. What do you know about your own temperament, personality, gifting, abilities, and passions? What does your personal profile say about how you might (and might not) be effective in expressing the gospel at work?

18. If you were to write a history of your faith journey, what significant events would you include? How has your spiritual background uniquely shaped your desire and ability to live out the gospel at work?

19. How would you characterize the work you do and the organization (or industry or profession or trade) within which you do it? What does this suggest about how you can tailor your attempts to live out the gospel?

20. How many bottom lines does your organization care about and track?

21. Does your organization embrace grace and truth, or do you tend toward one or the other?

22. Have you ever been a part of an organization that tried to coerce enthusiasm about a campaign, project, or program? Did it work? How many resources were wasted as a result? How can your organization grow in stewardship?

23. In your organization, are you more competitive or more collaborative? What is the last example you saw of collaboration benefiting the common good?

24. How does your organization treat its employees? How does it pay them, care for them, and develop them? Does your organization "love" its workers?

25. Is your organization one of the great ones in reflecting the beauty and goodness of the gospel? Or is it way down the list? Why?

26. What are the particulars of your organization that affect what it can do (and cannot do) in expressing the gospel?

27. Which region is your company in? What role can you play to ensure that your company is leveraging the gospel's reach, power, and intent for good?

28. How could a gospel focus correct a problem in your department, division, company, or industry?

29. How big is your vision for what your organization can accomplish in helping to renew the world?

ACKNOWLEDGMENTS

I have never produced a single good thought that wasn't shaped by others. I might not be able to cite the moment of the outside influence, but it was there. Likewise, I have been producing content in some form or fashion for over twenty-five years with the constant help of others.

Every book project, for me, is laced with strategic conversations with experts on the topic. Thanks to Bill, Greg, Donnie, Doug, Mike, Henry, Susie, Michael, Dave, Ted, Eric, Elise, Don, Johanna, Rob, and Brad for the inspiring conversations around this topic. For me, as a verbal processor, each of you fed my curiosity with your angle to this discussion.

Thanks to Andrew, Sean, Jason, Devin, Donna, Celeste, Elisabeth, and Kenny for help in research, writing, editing, layout, and administration that all combine to produce a project like this.

NOTES

Chapter 1: God's Big Canvas

1. Quoted in Nancy Pearcey, *Total Truth: Liberating Christianity from its Cultural Captivity* (Wheaton, IL: Crossway, 2004), 17.

2. Vincent van Gogh, letter to his brother, Theo, quoted at *http://www.brainyquote.com/quotes/quotes/v/vincentvan132735.html*.

3. Matthew 5:13, NIV.

4. Matthew 5:14-16, NIV.

5. 2 Corinthians 2:15-16, NIV.

6. Matthew 13:33, NIV.

Chapter 2: The Gospel and Your Job

1. Quoted in Nancy Pearcey, *Total Truth: Liberating Christianity from its Cultural Captivity* (Wheaton, IL: Crossway, 2004), 17.

2. Colossians 3:23-24, NIV.

3. For more on this concept, see Gabe Lyons, "Influencing Culture," *http://old.qideas.org/essays/influencing-culture.aspx*. Other writers and theologians besides Gabe and I have described the four acts of the gospel.

4. Pearcey, *Total Truth*, 48.

5. Quoted in Steven Garber, "Vocation Needs No Justification," *Comment*, September 1, 2010, *http://www.cardus.ca/comment/article/2357/vocation-needs-no-justification/*.

6. Ibid.

Chapter 3: Why Faith at Work Matters

1. Dorothy Sayers, "Why Work?" in *Letters to a Diminished Church: Passionate Arguments for the Relevance of Christian Doctrine* (Nashville: Thomas Nelson, 2004), 118.

2. Genesis 3:17-19, NIV.

3. Genesis 1:27-28, NIV.

4. Genesis 2:15, NIV.

5. Lydia Saad, "The '40-Hour' Workweek Is Actually Longer—by Seven Hours," Gallup, August 29, 2014, *http://www.gallup.com/poll/175286/hour-workweek-actually-longer-seven-hours.aspx*.

6. "Charts from the American Time Use Survey," Bureau of Labor Statistics, *http://www.bls.gov/tus/charts/*.

7. See *http://www.fastcompany.com/section/generation-flux*.

8. 1 Corinthians 9:22-23, NIV.

9. The following material is adapted from Stephen R. Graves and Thomas G. Addington, *The Fourth Frontier: Exploring the New World of Work* (Nashville: Word, 2000), 9–10.

Chapter 4: The Baseline and the Blue Sky

1. A. W. Tozer, *The Pursuit of God* (reprint, Las Vegas, NV: IAP, 2009), 75.

2. Luke 3, MSG.

3. Mark 7:24-30; Matthew 12:41; Matthew 8:5-13; Luke 17:11-19.

4. Martin Luther, *On the Babylonian Captivity of the Church* in *Three Treatises* (Philadelphia: Fortress Press, 1943), 201.

5. Pamela Rose Williams, "Top 24 Hudson Taylor Quotes," What Christians Want to Know, *http://www.whatchristianswanttoknow.com/top-24-hudson-taylor-quotes/*.

Chapter 5: A Purpose-Driven Job

1. Martin Luther, *An Open Letter to the Christian Nobility* in *Three Treatises* (Philadelphia, Fortress Press: 1943), 9.

2. Some of this material in this chapter is adapted from John C. Maxwell, Stephen R. Graves, and Thomas G. Addington, *Life@Work: Marketplace Success for People of Faith* (Nashville: Thomas Nelson, 2005). This book brings together many of the principles we put forward in the *Life@Work* magazine and our Promise Keepers talks. I recommend the Life@Work book if you want to read further about the individual baseline.

3. Regi Campbell, *About My Father's Business: Taking Your Faith to Work* (Colorado Springs, CO: Multnomah, 2005), 19.

4. Friedrich Nietzsche, *http://www.brainyquote.com/quotes/quotes/f/friedrichn103819.html*.

5. Os Guinness, *The Call: Finding and Fulfilling the Central Purpose of Your Life* (Thomas Nelson: Nashville, 2003), 7.

6. David Brooks, *The Road to Character* (New York: Random House, 2015), xi.

7. Dorothy Sayers, "Why Work?" in *Letters to a Diminished Church: Passionate Arguments for the Relevance of Christian Doctrine* (Nashville: Thomas Nelson, 2004), 132.

8. Matthew 25:14-15, NIV.

9. Booker T. Washington, *http://www.brainyquote.com/quotes/quotes/b/bookertwa382201.html*.

10. Bob Moawad, *http://www.goodreads.com/quotes/200343-help-others-get-ahead-you-will-always-stand-taller-with*.

11. Robert K. Greenleaf, *On Becoming a Servant-Leader*, ed. Don M. Frick and Larry C. Spears (New York: Paulist Press, 1977), 31.

12. Matthew 5:13-16, NIV.

Chapter 6: Gospel Entrepreneurship

1. Miroslav Volf, "The Church's Great Malfunctions," in *Engaging the Culture* (Nashville: Thomas Nelson, 2005), 105.

2. 1 Samuel 17:38-50, NIV.

3. The spiritual gifts include exhortation, giving, leadership, mercy, prophecy, service, teaching, administration, apostleship, discernment, faith, healing, helps, knowledge, miracle working, tongues, tongues interpretation, wisdom, evangelism, and pastoring. See Romans 12:3-8, 1 Corinthians 12:4-11, and Ephesians 4:7-13.

4. Studs Terkel, *Working: People Talk About What They Do All Day and How They Feel About What They Do* (New York: Pantheon, 1974).

5. Brian Dijkema, "The Work of Our Hands," *Cardus*, February 12, 2015, *http://www.cardus.ca/comment/article/4411/the-work-of-our-hands/*.

6. Quoted in Steven Garber, *Visions of Vocation: Common Grace for the Common Good* (Downers Grove, IL: InterVarsity Press, 2014), 146.

Chapter 7: Embedding the Gospel

1. D. Martyn Lloyd-Jones, *Studies in the Sermon on the Mount* (London: Inter-Varsity Press, 1960), 2:224.

2. See Stephen R. Graves, "The Defying Power of a MBL (Multiple Bottom Line)," June 2, 2014, *http://www.stephenrgraves.com/mbl/*.

3. Genesis 1:26, 28, NIV.

4. Genesis 2:15, NIV.

5. Genesis 1:27, NIV.

6. See Stephen R. Graves, "The Three Competencies of Generosity," Chapter 4 in *The Business of Generosity* (Fayetteville, AR: KJK, 2014). In this chapter I argue that generosity must sit on a three-legged stool— doing good, staying viable (the profit piece), and remaining true to its mission—if it's going to have longevity and authenticity.

7. See Stephen R. Graves, "The Fifth 'P,'" March 17, 2015, *http://www. stephenrgraves.com/the-fifth-p/*.

8. Simon Sinek, *Start with Why: How Great Leaders Inspire Everyone to Take Action* (New York: Penguin, 2009), back material.

9. Stephen R. Graves, "Meet Will & Chris Haughey & Tegu," February 12, 2014, *http://www.stephenrgraves.com/meet-will-chris-haughey-tegu/*.

10. Peter Block, *Stewardship: Choosing Service over Self-Interest* (San Francisco: Berrett-Koehler, 1993), xx.

11. Stephen R. Graves, "Should Money be Protected at all Costs?" 2015, *http://www.stephenrgraves.com/articles/read/should-money-be-protected-at-all-costs*.

12. Stephen R. Graves, "Why Should People Follow Your Lead?" 2015, *http://www.stephenrgraves.com/articles/read/why-should-people-follow-your-lead*.

13. Dan Sanker, *Collaborate! The Art of We: Combining Capabilities to Create New Opportunities for Success* (San Francisco: Jossey-Bass, 2012), 3.

14. Ed Catmull, "How Pixar Fosters Collective Creativity," *Harvard Business Review*, September 2008, https://hbr.org/2008/09/how-pixar-fosters-collective-creativity.

15. Jacob Morgan, "The 12 Habits of Highly Collaborative Organizations," *Forbes*, July 30, 2013, *http://www.forbes.com/sites/jacobmorgan/2013/07/30/the-12-habits-of-highly-collaborative-organizations/1/*.

16. Sanker, *Collaborate!* 73.

17. "Coaching," Stephen R. Graves, *http://www.stephenrgraves.com/coaching*.

18. Charles Handy, *The Hungry Spirit: Beyond Capitalism: A Quest for Purpose in the Modern World* (New York: Broadway, 1998), 171.

19. Henry Kaestner, "Work/Life Balance in Business: The Story of Bandwidth.com," Work as Worship Network, January 14, 2013, *http://www.workasworshipnetwork.org/worklife-balance-in-business-the-story-of-bandwidth-com/*.

Chapter 8: Extraordinary Organizations

1. G. K. Chesterton, *The Everlasting Man* (reprint, EMP Books, 2012), 82.

2. "Standard Occupational Classification," Bureau of Labor Statistics, *https://www.bls.gov/soc/*.

3. "Over 12,000 Job Descriptions," CareerPlanner.com, *https://dot-job-descriptions.careerplanner.com*.

4. John Calvin, *Commentary on Luke*, Luke 10:38.

5. Don Flow, "Don Flow on Flow Automotive," *https://www.youtube.com/watch?v=HEQ0kR3mrVA*.

6. Quoted by Eric Savitz in "Jack Dorsey: Leadership Secrets of Twitter and Square," *Forbes*, October 17, 2012, *http://www.forbes.com/sites/ericsavitz/2012/10/17/jack-dorsey-the-leadership-secrets-of-twitter-and-square/2/*.

Chapter 9: Both-and

1. Os Guinness, *The Call: Finding and Fulfilling the Central Purpose of Your Life* (Nashville: Thomas Nelson, 1998), 157.

2. Charles Colson, preface to William Wilberforce's *A Practical View of Christianity* (Peabody, MA: Hendrickson Classics, 1996), xii.

3. Robert Briner, *Roaring Lambs: A Gentle Plan to Radically Change Your World* (Grand Rapids, MI: Zondervan, 1995), 56.

THE BUSINESS OF GENEROSITY:
How Companies, Nonprofits, and Churches are Working
Together to Deliver Remarkable Good

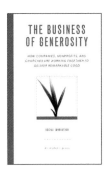

In *The Business of Generosity* you will:

- Learn what is driving young entrepreneurs to move beyond the single bottom line
- Develop a framework for leading your company to stay profitable, do good, and remain true to your mission all in harmony
- Discover how churches, business, and communities are working together to deliver remarkable good
- Construct language to articulate the "why" of what you do
- Become more intentional and strategic with the giving you do as a business and as an individual

MANAGING ME:

Why Some Leaders Build a Remarkable Legacy and Others Sadly Crumble

In *Managing Me* you will:

+ Better understand why self-leadership is so hard
+ Marry the ambition of leading your company and leading yourself
+ Be introduced to a model of sustainable leadership
+ Identify the critical gauges that steer your life and work progress
+ Create a filter to help sort the things that matter most

STRATEGY 3.0:
A Guide for Entrepreneurs, Millennials, Frustrated 5-year
Planners and Anyone Else Searching for Fast, Focused, and
Agile Strategy

In *Strategy 3.0* you will:

+ Learn why operating in old frameworks from an outdated
  perspective is such a costly mistake for leaders
+ Improve your ability to pivot and take advantage of market
  opportunities
+ Set your next company horizon and feel confident about
  reaching it
+ Encounter the fifteen critical terms and phrases that
  have become the working vocabulary of fast yet adaptive
  strategy
+ Develop and refine an eye that can extract the insights that
  are the foundation of all effective strategy

FLOURISHING:
Why Some People Thrive and Others Just Survive

In *Flourishing* you will:

+ Learn how to balance the competing demands of life and work
+ Unearth eight insights that anchor those who flourish most
+ Discover the kind of life you were designed to enjoy
+ See the value of slowing down (and what to actually do when you slow down)
+ Identify your true voice—the sound that your life makes when operating in its strike zone

THE HERO LEADER:
Why Effective Leaders Combine Strengths and Weaknesses

In *The Hero Leader* you will:
+ Understand the seven collective skill sets that all great leaders and managers develop
+ Learn how to become a legacy leader that others love to follow
+ Pinpoint what your team needs to develop and to lift their leadership horizon
+ See the opposite side of your core strengths and what the dangers are of ignoring those weaknesses
+ Consider how to staff in light of your personal skill set

ABOUT THE AUTHOR

Dr. Stephen R. Graves is a strategist, executive coach, and author. At any given time he is working with a handful of remarkable executives leading large global organizations and young social entrepreneurs just starting out. Steve has authored over a dozen books aimed at teaching people how to flourish in their life and work. When Steve is not consulting or writing on strategy, leadership, or impact, you can find him back-casting in the cold clear rivers of northwest Arkansas.

For more resources from KJK Inc. Publishing, go to *stephenrgraves.com.*